The 10 Sea

GRIMSBY TOWN

Seasons 1983-84 to 1992-93

Season-by-Season Commentary
Rob Briggs

Statistics and History
Mike Ross

Editors
Michael Robinson, John Robinson & Philip Norminton

CONTENTS

British Library Cataloguing in Publication Data
A catalogue record for this book is available from the British Library
ISBN 0-947808-29-9

Copyright © 1993; SOCCER BOOK PUBLISHING LTD. (0472-696226)
72, St. Peters' Avenue, Cleethorpes, Sth. Humberside, DN35 8HU, England

Printed by Adlard Print & Typesetting Services, The Old School, The Green, Ruddington, Notts. NG11 6HH

GRIMSBY TOWN FIRSTS by Mike Ross

In 1912, Bob Lincoln, in his book 'Reminiscences of Sport in Grimsby' graphically described the origins of the game in the town. He wrote of 'street football' with hordes of players and goals incredibly far apart - one end in Pasture Street and the other in King Street off Cleethorpe Road! Contrary to local belief, apparently, football was a later developer in the town and well-established teams were playing in Spilsby, Lincoln, Grantham, Brigg and even Louth for some time before Grimsby got its act together in the 1870's. Then, there were three local teams of note, Pelham, White Star and Wanderers who vied for local prominence. Pelham played just beyond Phelps Street in 'New Cleethorpes', White Star played on an adjacent field (after initially playing on the sands) and the Wanderers played on a piece of pasture land 'over the Marsh' next to the site of the future Grimsby and District Hospital.

Grimsby Pelham FC was formed by the members of the Worsley Cricket Club on 20th September 1878 when, meeting at the Wellington Arms in Freeman Street, they elected C. Horn (later to become headmaster of Welholme School) as their club captain. The club strip was blue and white hoops and the only games played in the 1878-79 season (due to the severe winter) were against Brigg Brittania.

Grimsby Pelham F.C., 1878

(pictured in Blue & White Hoops)
Left to Right - W.T. Lammin, R.C. Hall, Bob Lincoln, G. Atkinson, H. Evans, W. Ashling, A.H. Read
S. Noble, J. Warner, T. Atkinson, H. Monument, J. Fanthorpe

The 1879-80 season saw the club's name change to Grimsby Town and the fixture list grew to 15 matches with the following statistical tally : -

P W D L F A
15 6 3 6 21 15

In 1881/82 came the formation of the Lincolnshire FA and the inauguration of the Lincolnshire Cup. Town's first truly competitive game under the auspices of the Lincs FA was against Brigg Ancholme on 14th January 1882 and resulted in a 6-3 win.

In 1882, Town entered the FA Cup (then known as the English Cup) for the first time and drew the mighty Scottish side, Queens Park, at home. The Scots, however, not relishing the long railway journey, withdrew and Town's first opponents in the competition became the Rotherham steelworks side, Phoenix Bessemer. Played at Clee Park on 25th November 1882, this game ended in a 1-9 defeat with Harry Monument scoring Town's first FA Cup goal. On 3rd November 1883 Town faced Hull Town in their first away game in the FA Cup and recorded their first win in the competition with a 3-1 scoreline before losing to Grantham in the next round.

1884 saw the first of a number of changes in the club's colours when the blue and white hooped jerseys were exchanged for chocolate and blue quarters and, the following year saw the first FA Cup hat tricks when both Harry Monument (4) and J. Seal achieved the feat in an 8-0 thrashing of Darlington.

Grimsby Town F.C., 1887

Left to Right - H. Atkinson, J.H. Taylor, H. Smith, R. Chapman, H. Taylor, W.T. Lammin
H. Monument, J. Lee, R. McBeth, J. Lundie, W. Hopewell, L. Cooper
D. Riddock, H. Smith Jnr.   (all pictured in Chocolate & Blue Halves)

Town missed out when the Football League was formed in 1888 and, instead, joined 'The Combination', an organisation of Midlands and Lancashire clubs. Due to poor administration, this folded before the end of the season and, for the 1889/90 season, Town joined the newly-formed 'Football Alliance' and moved to Blundell Park. This proved highly successful and, after three seasons, member clubs were accepted 'en bloc' to form the Second Division of the Football League. By this time Town had moved to the Abbey Park (next to 'Peoples Park' where Legsby Avenue now stands) and on 3rd September 1892 the visitors for the first home game (which ended in a 2-1 victory) were Northwich Victoria. Town fared well in the 2nd Division finishing 4th, 5th, 9th, 3rd and 3rd in their first five seasons and in 1900/01 became champions and achieved promotion to the First Division. Two seasons later they were back in the Second Division and at the end of the 1909/10 season failed to be re-elected to the League when they finished second from bottom.

Dropping down to the Midland League, Town faced stiff opposition but, nevertheless, won the 1910/11 season Championship and, faring well in the FA Cup were rewarded by resuming their Second Division status for the 1911/12 season. After the disruption of the 1st World War, Town finished 22nd at the end of the 1919/20 season and only avoided the drop into Non-League football because the 3rd Division was formed by the mass defection of the Southern League clubs to the Football League. This meant that Town had no local games at all in 1920-21 and, when the 3rd Division North was formed the following year, Town were relieved to be transferred over.

After winning the Championship in 1925-26, Town made a welcome return to the 2nd Division and, three seasons later, were even promoted to the 1st Division for a further three years before dropping back in 1932-33. The following year Town won the 2nd Division Championship and embarked upon a 14-season spell in the 1st Division (during 1940-46 there was no competition because of the Second World War).

Since 1948/49, the club's history has continued to be a succession of highs and lows with 17 seasons of 2nd Division football, 20 seasons of 3rd Division football and just 7 seasons of 4th Division football. Add to those statistics the fact that during that time Town have been relegated and promoted seven times and have just 'avoided the drop' or just 'missed promotion' on many other occasions and the 'joys' of supporting this club become self-evident!

CLUB FIRSTS

First Game	**First F.A. Cup Scorer**
as Grimsby Pelham, 1st November 1879 vs Louth	Harry Monument
FC - score 1-1 (Louth equalised in last minute)	**First Hat-Trick**
	1st October 1892 vs Small Heath
First F.A. Cup Game & Defeat	Scored by Higgins (top scorer with 9 goals)
25th November 1882 vs Phoenix Bessemer (a) -	**First F.A. Cup Win**
score 1-9 (2nd round game as first round tie vs	3rd November 1883 vs Hull Town (a) - score 3-1
Queen's Park was scratched)	(Farnham, Noble 2)

CLUB FIRSTS

First F.A. Cup Draw
25th October 1884 vs Grantham (a) - score 1-1
(Mundahl)

First F.A. Cup Semi-Final
1935-36 vs Arsenal - score 0-1

First League Game & First League Victory
3rd September 1892 vs Northwich Victoria -
score 2-1

First League Scorer
Davie Riddoch (2)

First League Draw
18th February 1893 vs Lincoln City - score 2-2

First League Defeat
10th September 1892 vs Crewe - score 0-1

First League Cup Match & Defeat
26th October 1960 vs Bolton Wanderers (a) -
score 2-6 on aggregate (1st leg score 1-1)

First League Cup Scorer
Rafferty vs Bolton Wanderers

First League Cup Win
23rd September 1964 vs Oldham Athletic (h) -
score 3-1 on aggregate (1st leg score 2-1)

First League Cup Draw
17th November 1965 vs West Ham United (h) -
score 2-2 on aggregate (1st leg score 1-1)

First 2nd Division Championship
1900/1901 Season (Played 34 Points 49)

First 3rd Division Championship
1925/1926 Season (Played 42   Points 61)
(Note: 3rd Division North Championship)

First 4th Division Championship
1971/1972 Season (Played 46   Points 63)

An interesting first for Grimsby is Jack Swain. After making 22 First Division appearances for Grimsby between 1937 and 1939, he became the first ex-professional Football League player to become a Football League referee. Jack achieved this distinction when he was put on to the Football League list for the 1955/56 season.

Left: A photo of Jack Swain in his playing days

6

GRIMSBY TOWN SEASON 1983-84

After two mediocre seasons, Grimsby's 1983-84 campaign turned out to be the club's best since leaving the First Division in 1948. A final fifth place in Division Two was achieved with only the barest of squads and low gates, yet despite these obstacles, the quality of football witnessed was of the highest standard.

The difference was due to the astute signings of winger Paul Emson (Derby County) and veteran defender Chris Nicholl (Southampton), with the latter also doubling up as assistant-manager to Dave Booth. Emson's electric pace down the flanks was to provide the missing support for both Paul Wilkinson and Kevin Drinkell, particularly at home where Town were to lose only twice, remaining unbeaten at Blundell Park until Portsmouth's exciting 4-3 win in March. Earlier, a 2-1 victory at Derby in October had ended an away 'jinx', this being the Mariners' first away success for some thirteen months!

Wins at Chelsea (3-2) and Newcastle (1-0) helped achieve an unbeaten run of sixteen games, but after that Portsmouth defeat, the resulting tension brought a spell of inconsistency, with just one point gained from the Easter programme. For the second year in succession, the Divisional Champions - this time Chelsea - concluded the league season at Blundell Park, signing off with a 1-0 win before an above-average crowd of 13,000. Town's final line-up also put the accent on youth with the inclusion of Andy Moore and Gary Lund, both recent members of the club's Northern Intermediate League winning side.

GRIMSBY TOWN SEASON 1984-85

A fall to tenth position in the league was partly offset by progress in both Cup competitions, earning Grimsby national media attention. In the FA Cup, an excellent Gary Lund hat-trick helped defeat Notts County in a Third Round Replay, followed by a home tie in Round Four vs. Watford, before 'Match of the Day' cameras. The visitors included future Mariner Jimmy Gilligan, and it was his goal which contributed to an eventual 1-3 scoreline.

But it was in the Milk Cup where Town achieved the greater glory. After beating Barnsley over two legs, and Rotherham 6-1 after a replay, the Fourth Round took the Mariners to Everton, who themselves were destined to become League Champions. For 89 minutes the home side tried and failed to break the Grimsby rearguard, until a late free-kick allowed Paul Wilkinson to head home for a famous victory. Despite a 0-1 reverse against Norwich in the Quarter-Finals, for Wilkinson that memorable goal was to have a lasting effect, as a £300,000 transfer to Goodison Park was secured later in the season.

Once again, Town remained in contention for promotion without actually recording a consistent run of good results. Nevertheless, 72 league goals showed the quality of forwards Wilkinson, Drinkell and Lund (all incidentally, local-born), with some big scores achieved in several games. And, in March, Grimsby's 6-3 success over Cardiff marked their biggest league win of the past decade, on a day when both defences were equally suspect.

GRIMSBY TOWN SEASON 1985-86

With funds further boosted from the sale of Kevin Drinkell to Norwich, the club then made an all-out attempt for promotion by paying record fees of over £100,000 for Watford striker Jimmy Gilligan, and Leicester midfielder Andy Peake. However, as the season progressed, it was another summer buy - Gordon Hobson from Lincoln City - who made the greater impression, finishing the campaign as top scorer with 15 goals.

Town's poor showing was largely due to individuals not performing as a team (the first league win was not achieved until mid-September), leading in turn to a lack of spectator interest, plus a change of management. When Dave Booth resigned to go into business abroad, the club suffered further embarrassment when Liverpool's Phil Neal rejected the player-manager's post, with the directors then offering the position to Mike Lyons of Sheffield Wednesday. Whatever Lyons' qualities as a motivator and public relations man, this was to be no substitute for managerial experience, and later, some of his team selections were criticised by both press and public alike.

From a playing view, the highlight of the campaign was the exciting FA Cup tie vs. Arsenal, that was also beamed 'live' to Scandinavia. Youth again was given a chance in midfielder Mark Hine and defender Tony Barratt, although both were surprisingly released despite good showings in the first team. But undoubtedly the season belonged to Gordon Hobson, who showed that he could perform successfully at a higher grade of football.

Grimsby vs Barnsley (Division 2)   27th September 1986   -   Player-Manager Mike Lyons in an aerial battle.
Looking on for Barnsley are future Mariners Jim Dobbin (left) and Paul Futcher (right)

GRIMSBY TOWN SEASON 1986-87

In the summer of 1986, Mike Lyons' prediction of Division One football was further enhanced when he set a 100-goal target for promotion. Events however, were to prove him wrong on both counts, for despite being in a promising eighth position in March, relegation - and his subsequent dismissal - were the consequences.

With 31 players used during the season, lack of a settled team was clearly evident in several games as the manager changed his selections on a regular basis. Whilst injuries to a certain extent were to blame, the chosen replacements were themselves inexperienced and unlikely to benefit from playing in a struggling team, resulting in only ten wins achieved over the season. Morale wasn't helped either by the transfers of Andy Peake and Gordon Hobson, the latter especially so when he walked out on the club to join Southampton, despite having received two wage rises beforehand.

Indeed, Lyons' transfer dealings allowed Grimsby fans to see some talented players at Blundell Park. Welsh International Ian Walsh contributed a good scoring average before injury struck, while loan signings Des Hazel (Sheffield Wednesday) and Brian Rice (Nottingham Forest) temporarily added some class in midfield. But it was the sale of Kevin Moore to Oldham in February which was to alter the course of Town's season. With Lyons himself unavailable through injury, defence was left short on experience at a crucial time, with a number of 0-1 defeats eventually adding to the Mariners' downfall.

Paul Agnew in action 1987-88 season.
Grimsby's most consistent player of the past decade, having appeared in each of the last ten seasons.

GRIMSBY TOWN SEASON 1987-88

With Town's return to Division Three football ending in a second successive relegation, the season became notable for events off the pitch as well as on it. As finances started to bite, the decision to increase share capital to £600,000 was followed by the resignation of Chairman Ron Ramsden, whilst later, when a £30,000 tax bill threatened the club's very existence, it was only two appeal funds which allowed its continuation.

For new manager Bobby Roberts, Blundell Park offered a 'no-win' situation. Relegation from Division Two saw a significant drop in interest from both sponsors and supporters, and, with no money to strengthen an already depleted squad, new arrivals were limited to loan players and trialists. Although one of the former - Marc North from Luton Town - was to finish as top scorer after signing permanently with 11 goals, he was also to prove both 'hero' and 'villain'. In the penultimate game at Wigan, his lone strike offered hope against relegation, but when Aldershot visited in the final match, a vital penalty miss was to ensure Fourth Division soccer.

Some of the Mariners' early performances are best left forgotten, but after Christmas, the signing of Shaun Cunnington and Kevin Jobling led to an improvement in results. Too many drawn games however, were to keep Grimsby in the relegation zone, and once confirmed, it seemed a particularly unjust reward for Don O'Riordan. At times an outstanding player, his contribution was recognised when the 'Sunday People' voted him the Division's top defender.

Marc North salutes the crowd after scoring as Steve Saunders rushes to celebrate.
1987-88 Season.

10

GRIMSBY TOWN SEASON 1988-89

When Alan Buckley became Grimsby's third manager in just twelve months, the team had to be rebuilt virtually from scratch. With money again unavailable, Buckley relied on graduates from the youth side and arrivals from non-league football, and although combining well later in the season, some supporters still thought that a further drop into the Vauxhall Conference was possible.

After Marc North had redeemed himself by scoring the first goal at home vs. Torquay (earning himself a £50 sponsors prize in the process), Grimsby then seemed to justify the pessimists' view by hovering above the relegation area. Gradually, team understanding got better, and when a catalyst was needed to restore the fans' confidence, the FA Cup was to provide it. Local hero John Cockerill's goal secured an unexpected victory over Wolves in Round One, and after accounting for Rotherham, Town upset the form book once more by beating First Division Middlesbrough 2-1 at Ayresome Park. Further success over Reading meant a Fifth Round visit to Cup holders Wimbledon, but despite an early lead, the Dons' physical style eventually gave them the tie.

Building on the support at Wimbledon - when 6,000 fans and as many 'Harry Haddocks' made the journey - the Mariners steadily climbed the table. However, a crucial 2-3 defeat at Tranmere (the only one in the last nine games) brought a final position of ninth, restoring hope for the future. Although promotion wasn't achieved, at least the Conference seemed a lot further off than nine months before.

GRIMSBY TOWN SEASON 1989-90

Grimsby's Fourth Division promotion season never really got underway until mid-November, when the inspired signing of Garry Birtles earned both points at Wrexham to begin the climb from 17th place in the league. Afterwards, only five games were lost, allowing the Mariners to claim second spot behind champions Exeter City.

Not that the previous three months of the campaign weren't also eventful. In September, newcomers Maidstone United claimed their first-ever away success in the league when winning at Blundell Park, whilst in the League Cup, Town accounted for Hull City thanks to a last-minute strike by Gary Childs in extra-time. Round Two then brought Coventry City to Cleethorpes, and in a traditional Cup-tie atmosphere, Grimsby finished as 3-1 victors. The second leg however was somewhat disappointing, as following Tony Rees' early dismissal, it was left to former Mariner Kevin Drinkell to set Coventry on the road to a 3-0 win.

In the New Year Keith Alexander established a club record by scoring in three successive matches (vs. Carlisle, York and Maidstone) when appearing as a substitute, whilst the month of March firmly put the Mariners on course for promotion with a 100% points return from seven games. But overall, the best performance was reserved for the final home match against Wrexham. On a hot sunny day, Garry Birtles - a free transfer arrival - emphasised his class and ability by hitting a hat-trick, going on to also claim a deserved 'Player Of The Year' award.

GRIMSBY TOWN SEASON 1990-91

By contrast, Town's second successive promotion campaign bore the hallmark of consistency. Never out of the top three places from start to finish, a final third position created another record, as both Southend and Cambridge likewise accompanied them from Divisions Four to Two.

With early exits from both major Cup competitions, Grimsby were able to concentrate solely on the league. Several teams were to face the wrath of a resurgent Mariners' front line, including Preston (twice) and Rotherham, whilst vs. Bournemouth just before Christmas, there was a five-goal feast in store at Blundell Park. For the second year running, three goalscorers ended the season in double figures, but despite their contribution, defender Paul Futcher was to prove the most inspired team selection. Signed on loan in January after Andy Tillson's record move to QPR, his subsequent transfer brought experience at a crucial time, and earnt him a first-ever taste of promotion.

Grimsby's only real concern was a lack of goals towards the seasons' end, but thankfully everything came right for the last home game vs. Exeter City. Before one of Blundell Park's biggest crowds for several years, Cleethorpes-born John Cockerill confirmed his standing as a 'local hero' by scoring twice, although the visitors never game in, pulling a goal back and later hitting a post. Overall, a final placing of third merited an excellent achievement, even if the title itself would have been a more fitting reward for Town's style of play.

Grimsby Town F.C.   Season 1990-91 (Promoted to Division Two)
Back : Left to Right - P. Jellitt (Physio), C. Hargreaves, M. Lever, A. Tillson, I. Knight, S. Sherwood, P. Reece, K. Alexander, J. Cockerill, R. Willis, G. Birtles, A. Mann (Reserve Team Coach)
Front - P. Agnew, T. Rees, S. Cunnington, T. Watson, A. Buckley (Manager), G. Childs, J. McDermott, D. Gilbert, K. Jobling

GRIMSBY TOWN SEASON 1991-92

The excitement of Grimsby's opening Second Division fixture - when visitors Cambridge won 4-3 thanks to a last-minute goal - was to also mark the beginning of a frustrating season for the club. Almost every player suffered at some stage from injury to necessitate regular team changes, and coupled with varying fortunes on the pitch, it meant Town's outcome wasn't decided until the final game.

Undoubtedly, the player missed the most was John Cockerill, who made his last appearance in December's 3-1 success over Bristol City before injuries sustained in that game led to his eventual retirement. Without that extra 'bite' in midfield that had been the backbone of Grimsby's double promotion years, service to the forwards was not so great by comparison, although skipper Shaun Cunnington continued to lead the Mariners by example. The 3-1 win at Charlton in March still gave the club an outside chance of making the Play-Offs, but defeat in six of the last eight games (all by a 0-1 scoreline) brought relegation involvement instead.

The League Cup however, provided some relief with an excellent 1-1 draw at Aston Villa to take the tie on away goals, before Tottenham Hotspur (including Gary Lineker) emphasised the art of finishing by scoring from all three clear chances created. Back in Division Two, Tommy Watson's lone strike at Port Vale - his second of the season - not only ensured the Mariners' survival, but also meant he had scored both the first and last goals of Grimsby's campaign!

GRIMSBY TOWN SEASON 1992-93

Due to League reorganisation, Grimsby began the 1992-93 season in Division One, and after being widely tipped for relegation, ninth position at the finish was to prove doubly satisfying. At one stage it even seemed that a Play-Off spot might be achieved, but a total of fifteen away defeats - the most in the Division - meant Premier League status remained just a dream.

Whilst teams like Newcastle and Derby were prepared to spend millions on strengthening their squads, Alan Buckley paid a more modest £125,000 for Blackpool skipper Paul Groves to replace Sunderland-bound Shaun Cunnington. Similarly, Rhys Wilmot and Clive Mendonca arrived to boost other departments, while the success of the club's youth policy was shown with the emergence of defenders Gary Croft and Peter Handyside. Indeed, Handyside's form earned him a Scottish Under-21 cap after only five league games, adding to a Barclays League appearance by the evergreen Paul Futcher against Italy, with Paul Agnew also winning a call-up to the Northern Ireland squad.

Jim Dobbin's last-minute winner at eventual Champions Newcastle - the season's best result - coincided with the loan debut of goalkeeper Dave Beasant from Chelsea. Beasant's six-game spell included five wins to lift Grimsby to a healthier league position, with consistent form then maintained after Christmas. Despite playing good football though, one worrying aspect was the lack of support off the field; whilst a top ten placing might augur well for the future, average gates of around 5,000 do not.

1983-84

#	Date			Opponent	Res	Score	Scorers	Att
1	Aug	27	(h)	Shrewsbury T	D	1-1	Drinkell	5,177
2	Sep	3	(a)	Cardiff C	L	1-3	Waters	5,135
3		6	(h)	Leeds U	W	2-0	Drinkell, Waters (pen)	7,797
4		10	(h)	Newcastle U	D	1-1	Speight	9,000
5		17	(a)	Middlesbrough	D	1-1	Waters	10,239
6		24	(h)	Fulham	W	2-1	Wilkinson, Emson	5,769
7		27	(a)	Barnsley	L	1-3	Wilkinson	10,966
8	Oct	1	(a)	Manchester C	L	1-2	Emson	25,080
9		8	(a)	Huddersfield T	D	0-0		8,897
10		15	(h)	Brighton & HA	W	5-0	Wilkinson 2, Ford, Lund, Emson	5,969
11		22	(h)	Crystal P	W	2-0	Waters, Ford	6,075
12		29	(a)	Derby C	W	2-1	Drinkell 2	11,531
13	Nov	5	(a)	Portsmouth	L	0-4		12,906
14		12	(h)	Charlton A	W	2-1	Drinkell, Whymark	5,584
15		19	(a)	Swansea C	W	1-0	K.Moore	6,178
16		26	(h)	Carlisle U	D	1-1	Waters (pen)	5,665
17	Dec	4	(a)	Blackburn R	D	1-1	Bonnyman	6,409
18		13	(h)	Oldham A	W	3-0	Ford, Speight, Wilkinson	4,825
19		17	(a)	Chelsea	W	3-2	Waters, Emson, Ford	13,151
20		26	(h)	Sheffield W	W	1-0	Wilkinson	16,197
21		28	(a)	Cambridge U	D	2-2	Emson, Ford	4,319
22		31	(h)	Cardiff C	W	1-0	Emson	7,164
23	Jan	2	(a)	Fulham	D	1-1	Drinkell	7,351
24		14	(a)	Shrewsbury T	W	2-1	Drinkell, Wilkinson	3,343
25		21	(h)	Middlesbrough	D	0-0		7,342
26	Feb	4	(h)	Manchester C	D	1-1	Wilkinson	11,986
27		11	(a)	Newcastle U	W	1-0	Drinkell	28,526
28		21	(h)	Derby C	W	2-1	Wilkinson, Drinkell	8,530
29		25	(a)	Crystal P	W	1-0	Ford	5,956
30	Mar	3	(h)	Portsmouth	L	3-4	Drinkell, Ford, Cumming	8,729
31		10	(a)	Charlton A	D	3-3	Drinkell 2, Ford	7,626
32		17	(a)	Leeds U	L	1-2	Wilkinson	14,412
33		31	(h)	Huddersfield T	W	2-1	Waters (pen), Bonnyman	7,541
34	Apr	7	(a)	Brighton & HA	L	0-2		10,610
35		10	(h)	Barnsley	W	1-0	Wilkinson	6,769
36		14	(h)	Swansea C	W	3-0	Drinkell 3	5,851
37		21	(a)	Sheffield W	L	0-1		25,828
38		23	(h)	Cambridge U	D	0-0		5,828
39		28	(a)	Carlisle U	D	1-1	Wilkinson	3,512
40	May	5	(h)	Blackburn R	W	3-2	Bonnyman (pen), Lund 2	4,826
41		7	(a)	Oldham A	L	1-2	Lund	4,156
42		12	(h)	Chelsea	L	0-1		13,000

FINAL LEAGUE POSITION : 5th in Division Two

Appearances

Sub Appearances

Goals

14

Batch	Cumming	Crombie	Waters	Nicholl	Moore K	Ford	Wilkinson	Drinkell	Bonnyman	Emson	Speight	Whymark	Moore A	Cooper	Lund	Henshaw	Agnew	Shearer	№
1	2	3	4	5	6	7	8	9	10	11									1
1	2	3	4		6	7	8*	9	10	11		12		5					2
1		3	4	5	6	7		9	10	11		8		2					3
1		3	4	5	6	7		9		11	10	8		2					4
1		3	4	5	6	7	8	9		11	10			2					5
1	12	3	4	5	6	7	8	9*		11	10			2					6
1	12	3	4	5	6	7	9			11	10			2	8*				7
1	12	3	4*	5	6	7	8	9		11	10			2					8
1	2	3	4	5	6	7	8	9		11	10								9
1	2	3	4	5	6	7	9			11	10*				8	12			10
1	2	3	4	5	6	7	8	9	10	11									11
1	2	3	4	5	6	7	8	9		11	10								12
1	2	3	4	5	6	7		9		11*	10	12				8			13
1	2	3	4		6	7	8	9		11	10	5							14
1	2	3	4	5	6	7	8	9		11	10								15
1	2	3	4	5	6	7	8	9		11	10								16
1	2	3	4	5	6	7	8*	9	12	11	10								17
1	2	3	4	5	6	7	8		12	11	10*	9							18
1	2	3	4	5	6	7	8		10	11		9							19
1	3		4	5	6	7	8		10	11		9	2						20
1	3		4	5	6	7	8	12	10	11		9*	2						21
1	2	3	4	5	6	7		9	10	11		8							22
1	2	3	4	5	6	7		9	10	11		8							23
1		3	4	5	6	7	8	9	10	11			2						24
1	2	3	4	5	6	7	8	9	10	11									25
1	2*	3	4	5	6	7	8	9	10	11	12								26
1	2	3	4	5	6	7	8	9	10	11									27
1	2	3	4	5	6	7	8	9	10	11									28
1	2	3	4	5	6	7	8	9	10	11									29
1	2	3	4	5	6	7	8	9	10	11									30
1	2	3	4	5	6	7	8	9	10	11*	12								31
1		3	4	5	6	7	8	9	10	11	2								32
1		3	4	5	6	7	8	9	10	11			2						33
1		3	4	5	6	7	8*	9	10	11			2			12			34
1		3	4	5	6	7	8	9	10*	11	2					12			35
1		3	4	5	6	7	8	9	10	11*	2					12			36
1		3	4*	5	6	7	8		10	11	2	12			9				37
1	2	3		5	6*	7	8	9		11	4				12	10			38
1	2	3		5	6	7	8	9	10	11	4								39
1	2*	3			6	7	8	9	10		4			5	12	11			40
1	6		5			7	8	9	10		4		2		11		3		41
1		3		5	6	7	8	9	10		4		2		12	11*			42
42	27	40	37	39	41	42	37	35	27	39	23	9	8	7	4	3	1	1	
	3						1	2		2	2	1			3	1		3	
		1	7		1	8	12	15	3	6	2	1			4				

1984-85

1	Aug	25	(h)	Barnsley	W	1-0	Wilkinson	6,190
2		27	(a)	Manchester C	L	0-3		21,137
3	Sep	1	(a)	Middlesbrough	W	5-1	Drinkell 2, Emson, Wilkinson, Ford	5,179
4		4	(h)	Charlton A	W	2-1	Drinkell, Ford	5,692
5		8	(h)	Leeds U	L	0-2		13,290
6		15	(a)	Blackburn R	L	1-3	Wilkinson	5,203
7		22	(h)	Oxford U	L	1-2	Bonnyman	5,563
8		29	(a)	Sheffield U	W	3-2	Lund 3	12,438
9	Oct	6	(h)	Oldham A	W	4-1	Emson 2, Wilkinson, Foley	5,072
10		13	(a)	Portsmouth	L	2-3	Wilkinson 2	13,624
11		20	(h)	Carlisle U	W	1-0	Lund	4,832
12		27	(a)	Cardiff C	W	4-2	Lund, Wilkinson, Emson, Drinkell	4,500
13	Nov	3	(a)	Notts Co	D	1-1	K.Moore	5,750
14		10	(h)	Wolves	W	5-1	Wilkinson, Barnes (og), Ford, Bonnyman, Drinkell	7,220
15		17	(h)	Fulham	L	2-4	Ford, Lund	6,287
16		24	(a)	Wimbledon	D	1-1	K.Moore	3,314
17	Dec	1	(h)	Shrewsbury T	W	2-1	Wilkinson, Bonnyman	6,146
18		8	(a)	Brighton & HA	D	0-0		9,367
19		15	(h)	Crystal P	L	1-3	Wilkinson	5,814
20		22	(h)	Middlesbrough	W	3-1	K.Moore, Wilkinson, Drinkell	5,650
21		26	(a)	Birmingham C	L	1-2	Drinkell	14,168
22		29	(a)	Charlton A	L	1-4	K.Moore	3,853
23	Jan	1	(h)	Huddersfield T	W	5-1	Cumming 2, Lund, Foley, Wilkinson	8,790
24		12	(h)	Blackburn R	D	1-1	Lund	7,851
25	Feb	2	(h)	Sheffield U	L	0-2		7,261
26		9	(a)	Leeds U	D	0-0		12,517
27		23	(h)	Notts Co	W	2-0	Drinkell 2	4,966
28	Mar	2	(h)	Cardiff C	W	6-3	Bonnyman 2 (2 pens), Drinkell 2, Ford, Lund	4,285
29		5	(a)	Wolves	W	1-0	Ford	6,127
30		9	(a)	Carlisle U	D	1-1	Wilkinson	3,218
31		16	(h)	Portsmouth	L	2-3	Cumming, Wilkinson	6,197
32		23	(a)	Oldham A	L	0-2		3,388
33		30	(a)	Oxford U	L	0-1		8,587
34	Apr	5	(h)	Birmingham C	W	1-0	Henshaw (pen)	6,926
35		9	(a)	Huddersfield T	D	0-0		5,834
36		13	(h)	Manchester C	W	4-1	Drinkell, Lund 2, Cumming	8,362
37		20	(a)	Fulham	L	1-2	Lund	3,632
38		27	(h)	Wimbledon	W	2-1	Cumming, Bonnyman (pen)	4,283
39		30	(a)	Barnsley	D	0-0		3,261
40	May	4	(a)	Shrewsbury T	L	1-4	Bonnyman	3,450
41		7	(h)	Brighton & HA	L	2-4	Bonnyman, Matthews	4,034
42		•11	(a)	Crystal P	W	2-0	Drinkell 2	4,923

FINAL LEAGUE POSITION : 10th in Division Two

Appearances

Sub Appearances

Goals

16

Batch	Cumming	Crombie	Foley	Nicholl	Moore K	Ford	Lund	Wilkinson	Bonnyman	Emson	Drinkell	Seagraves	Robinson	Moore A	Felgate	Agnew	Hine	Henshaw	Grotier	Matthews	Rowbotham	Dawson	
1	2	3	4	5	6	7	8*	9	10	11	12												1
1	2*	3	4	5	6	7		8	10	11	9	12											2
1		3	4	5	6	7		8	10	11	9	2											3
1		3	4	5	6	7		8	10	11	9	2											4
1		3	4	5	6	7		8	10	11	9	2											5
1		3	4	5	6	7		8	10	11	9	2*						12					6
1		3	4	5	6	7	12	8	10		9	2						11*					7
1		3	4	5	6	7	9	8	10	11		2											8
1		3	4	5	6	7	9	8	10	11		2											9
1		3	4	5	6	7		8	10	11		2								9			10
1		3	4	5	6	7	9	8	10	11		2											11
1		5	4		6	7	9	8	10	11*	12	2				3							12
1			4	5	6	7	9*	8	10	11	12	2				3							13
1		3	4	5	6	7	9	8*	10	11	12	2											14
1		3	4	5	6	7	9	8	10	11	12	2*											15
1		3	4	5	6	7		8	10	11	9	2											16
1		3	4	5	6	7		8	10	11	9	2											17
1		3	4	5	6	7		8	10	11	9	2											18
1		3	4	5	6	7	12	8	10	11	9	2*											19
1			4	5	6	7	12	8*	10	11	9	2				3							20
1	12	3	4	5	6	7		8	10	11*	9	2											21
1	12	3	4	5	6	7		8	10	11	9*	2											22
1		5	4		6	7	9	8	10	11		2				3							23
		5	4		6	7	9	8	10	11		2				3			1				24
	12	5	4		6	7	9	8	10	11*		2				3			1				25
		3	4*		6	7	12	8	10	11	9	2	5								1		26
	12	3	4	5		7	8*		10	11	9	2	6		1								27
	12	3	4	5		7*	8		10	11	9	2	6		1								28
	11	3	4	5	6	7		8	10		9	2			1								29
	11	3	4	5	6*	7		8	10	12	9	2			1								30
	11	3	4	5	6*	7		8	10	12	9	2			1								31
	11	6		5		7	12	8			9	2			1	3	10*			4			32
	11	3		5		7	8				9	2	6		1	4	10						33
	11	3		5		7	8				9	2	6		1	4	10						34
	11*	3		5		7	8		12		9	2	6		1	4	10						35
	11	3		5		7	8				9	2	6		1	4	10						36
	11	3			6	7	8		10	12	9	2*	5		1	4							37
	11				6	7	8*		10	12	9	2	5		1	3	4						38
	11	6				7			10	8	9	2	5			3	4*		1	12			39
	11	6				7			10		9	2	5			3	12		1	8*	4		40
		6				7			10	11	9	2	5			3			1	8	4		41
	2	6				7			10	11	9		5			3	4		1	8			42
23	15	39	31	31	31	42	19	30	37	30	30	22	17	13	12	12	8	6	6	4	3	1	
	5					5			5	5	1						1	1		1			
	5		2		4	6	12	14	8	4	14							1		1			

17

1985-86

1	Aug	17	(a)	Brighton & HA	D	2-2	Lund, Hobson	9,787
2		20	(h)	Huddersfield T	D	1-1	Lund	6,180
3		24	(h)	Charlton A	D	2-2	Lund, Hobson	4,260
4		26	(a)	Fulham	L	1-2	Lund	4,873
5		31	(h)	Wimbledon	L	0-1		3,476
6	Sep	4	(a)	Stoke C	D	1-1	Lund	7,362
7		7	(a)	Sunderland	D	3-3	Ford, Gilligan, Lund	14,985
8		13	(h)	Carlisle U	W	1-0	Peake	4,099
9		21	(a)	Barnsley	L	0-1		5,356
10		28	(h)	Bradford C	W	2-0	Peake, Emson	5,158
11	Oct	5	(a)	Oldham A	L	1-2	Gilligan	5,301
12		12	(h)	Sheffield U	L	0-1		5,935
13		19	(a)	Leeds U	D	1-1	Hobson	11,244
14		26	(h)	Middlesbrough	W	3-2	Hobson, Gilligan 2	4,454
15	Nov	2	(h)	Millwall	W	5-1	Hobson 3, A.Moore, Bonnyman	3,658
16		9	(a)	Crystal P	L	1-2	Emson	4,620
17		16	(h)	Portsmouth	W	1-0	Bonnyman (pen)	6,436
18		23	(a)	Norwich C	L	2-3	Culverhouse (og), Emson	12,018
19		30	(h)	Blackburn R	W	5-2	Ford, Hine, A.Moore, Hobson 2	5,016
20	Dec	7	(a)	Huddersfield T	D	2-2	Lyons, Hobson	4,811
21		14	(h)	Brighton & HA	L	0-2		5,320
22		21	(a)	Charlton A	L	0-2		3,525
23		26	(a)	Hull C	L	0-2		12,824
24	Jan	1	(h)	Shrewsbury T	W	3-1	Lyons 2, Lund	4,750
25		11	(a)	Carlisle U	W	2-1	Hobson, Emson	2,483
26		18	(a)	Wimbledon	L	0-3		2,770
27		25	(h)	Stoke C	D	3-3	Emson, Bonnyman, Ford	4,523
28	Feb	1	(h)	Fulham	W	1-0	Peake	3,576
29		8	(h)	Leeds U	W	1-0	Hobson	6,382
30	Mar	1	(a)	Bradford C	W	1-0	Cumming	5,185
31		4	(a)	Middlesbrough	L	1-3	Crombie	4,496
32		8	(h)	Oldham A	L	1-4	Hobson	4,178
33		15	(a)	Sheffield U	D	1-1	Henshaw	9,165
34		22	(h)	Sunderland	D	1-1	Lund	5,339
35		29	(a)	Shrewsbury T	W	2-0	Lyons, Henshaw (pen)	3,097
36	Apr	1	(h)	Hull C	L	0-1		9,121
37		5	(a)	Millwall	L	0-1		3,612
38		12	(h)	Crystal P	W	3-0	Henshaw 2 (1 pen), Peake	4,222
39		19	(a)	Portsmouth	L	1-3	Cumming	12,967
40		22	(h)	Barnsley	L	1-2	Hobson	4,009
41		26	(h)	Norwich C	W	1-0	Hobson	8,090
42	May	5	(a)	Blackburn R	L	1-3	K.Moore	7,600

FINAL LEAGUE POSITION : 15th in Division Two

Appearances

Sub Appearances

Goals

18

Felgate	Robinson	Agnew	Peake	Moore A	Crombie	Ford	Lund	Gilligan	Bonnyman	Emson	Hobson	Moore K	Lyons	Cumming	Hine	Henshaw	Barratt	Batch	Matthews	Grocock	#
1	2	3	4	5	6	7	8	9	10	11*	12										1
1	2	3	4	5	6	7	8*	9	10	11	12										2
1	2	3	4	5		7	8	9	10	11	6										3
1	2	3	4	5	6	7	8	9	10	11*				12							4
1			4	5	3	7	8	9	10		11	6					2				5
1	2		4	5	3	7	8	9	10		11	6									6
1	2*		4	5	3	7	8	9	10	12	11	6									7
1	2*		4	5	3	7	8	9	10	12	11	6									8
1		3	4	5		7	8	12	10	11*	9	6					2				9
1		3	4	5		7		8		11	9	6			10		2				10
1		3	4	5		7	12	8		11*	9	6			10		2				11
			4	5	3	7*	12	8		11	9	6			10		2	1			12
			4	5	3*	7	12	8	10		9	6		11			2	1			13
			4	5	3	7		8	10	11	9	6					2	1			14
			4*	5	3	7		8	10	11	9	6		12			2	1			15
			4	5	3	7		8*	10	11	9	6		12			2	1			16
			4		3	7	8		10	11	9	6	5				2	1			17
		3	4			7	8		10	11	9	6	5				2	1			18
			4			7	8		10		9	6	5	3	11		2	1			19
	12		4			7	8*		10		9	6	5	3	11		2	1			20
			4		12	7	8*		10		9	6	5	3	11		2	1			21
			4		3	7	12		10	11*	9	6	5	8			2	1			22
			4		3	7	12		10		9	6	5*	11	8		2	1			23
		3				7	8		10		9	6	5	11	4		2	1			24
1		3	4		6	7	8	12		11	9		5	10*			2				25
		3	4		6	7*	8	12	10	11	9		5				2	1			26
	2		4		6	7	8		10	11	9		5	3				1			27
	2		4		6	7	8		10	11	9		5	3				1			28
	2		4		6	7	8*	12	10	11	9		5	3				1			29
	2	3	4	5	6	7			10	11	9			8				1			30
	2	3	4	5	6	7			10	11	9			8				1			31
	2	3	4		6	7			10*	11	9	12	5	8				1			32
	10		4	2	3	12	8				9	6	5	11*		7		1			33
	10		4	2	3	12	8				9	6	5	11		7*		1			34
	10	3	4	2			8				9	6	5	7*	11	12		1			35
			4	2	3		8				9	6	5	11	10	7*	12	1			36
	2		4	12	3		8					6	5	11	10	9*	7	1			37
	10		4	2	3		8				9	6	5	11*		7		1	12		38
	10	12	4	2	3		8*				9	6	5	11		7		1			39
	10		4	2	3		8*				9	6	5	11		7		1	12		40
	10		4	2	3		12				9	6	5	11		7		1	8*		41
	10		4		3			2			9	6	5	11*		7		1	8	12	42
12	22	14	36	31	33	32	24	19	29	21	39	30	24	22	12	10	20	30	2		
	2		1	1	2	5	5		2	2	1		2	1		2		2	1		
			4	1	1	3	8	4	3	5	15	2	4	2	1	4					

1986-87

1	Aug	23	(a)	Ipswich T	D	1-1	Walsh		12,455
2		30	(h)	Bradford C	D	0-0			6,393
3	Sep	6	(a)	Brighton & HA	W	1-0	Hobson		7,791
4		13	(h)	Derby Co	L	0-1			7,305
5		20	(a)	Sheffield U	W	2-1	Hobson, K.Moore		9,840
6		27	(h)	Barnsley	L	0-1			4,789
7	Oct	1	(a)	Reading	W	3-2	Henshaw, Turner, Walsh		6,130
8		4	(a)	Shrewsbury T	L	1-4	Walsh (pen)		2,451
9		11	(h)	Plymouth A	D	1-1	K.Moore		4,155
10		18	(a)	West Brom A	D	1-1	Rawcliffe		8,618
11		25	(h)	Leeds U	D	0-0			7,168
12	Nov	1	(h)	Millwall	W	1-0	K.Moore		3,757
13		8	(a)	Crystal P	W	3-0	Walsh, Hobson, O'Riordan		5,052
14		15	(h)	Sunderland	D	1-1	Walsh (pen)		7,065
15		22	(a)	Portsmouth	L	1-2	Hazel		9,517
16		29	(h)	Birmingham C	L	0-1			4,734
17	Dec	2	(h)	Blackburn R	W	1-0	O'Riordan		3,483
18		6	(a)	Hull C .	D	1-1	Hazel		7,217
19		13	(h)	Stoke C	D	1-1	Rawcliffe		4,642
20		21	(a)	Derby Co	L	0-4			14,440
21		26	(h)	Oldham A	D	2-2	O'Riordan, Henshaw		6,469
22		27	(a)	Sunderland	W	1-0	Walsh		13,769
23	Jan	1	(a)	Huddersfield T	D	0-0			7,530
24		3	(h)	Brighton & HA	L	1-2	Henshaw		4,729
25		17	(a)	Blackburn R	D	2-2	Walsh 2 (1 pen)		4,654
26		24	(h)	Ipswich T	D	1-1	Robinson		4,981
27	Feb	7	(a)	Bradford C	L	2-4	K.Moore 2		8,413
28		14	(h)	Reading	W	3-2	Robinson 2, Turner		3,579
29		24	(a)	Barnsley	L	0-1			5,136
30		28	(h)	Sheffield U	W	1-0	O'Riordan		5,051
31	Mar	7	(a)	Leeds U	L	0-2			14,270
32		14	(h)	West Brom A	W	3-1	Henshaw, O'Riordan, Cumming		5,024
33		21	(a)	Plymouth A	L	0-5			2,671
34		28	(h)	Shrewsbury T	L	0-1			3,437
35	Apr	4	(h)	Crystal P	L	0-1			3,071
36		11	(a)	Millwall	L	0-1			3,881
37		18	(h)	Huddersfield T	L	0-1			4,198
38		21	(a)	Oldham A	D	1-1	O'Riordan		7,032
39		25	(h)	Portsmouth	L	0-2			5,085
40	May	2	(a)	Birmingham C	L	0-1			4,457
41		5	(h)	Hull C	D	2-2	Walsh, Turner		6,757
42		9	(a)	Stoke C	L	1-5	McGarvey		6,407

FINAL LEAGUE POSITION : 21st in Division Two

Appearances

Sub Appearances

Goals

Batch	Burgess	Cumming	Peake	Lyons	Moore K	Robinson	Walsh	Hobson	O'Riordan	Turner	Agnew	Felgate	Prudhoe	Halsall	Crombie	Rawcliffe	Henshaw	Bonnyman	McDermott	McGarvey	Hazel	Straw	Rice	Grocock	Moore A	Horwood	Dixon	Matthews	Moore D	Pratt	
1	2	3	4	5	6	7	8	9	10	11																					1
1	2	3	4	5	6	7	8	9	10	11																					2
1	2	3	4	5	6		8	9	10	11							7*					12									3
1	2	12		5	6	4*	8	9	10	11					3		7														4
1	2			5	6		8	9	10	11	3						7					4									5
1	2	3	5				8	9*	10	11					6		7					4			12						6
1	2	3	5*			9	8		10	11					6	12	7					4									7
1	2	3				9	8		10	11					6	12	7					4*			5						8
1	2	3	5*	6			8	9	10	11						12	7	4													9
1	2		5*	6			8		10	11	3					9	7	12				4									10
	2			5	6		8	9	10		3	1				12	11*				7	4									11
	2			5	6			9	10		3	1				8					7	4	11								12
	2			5	6	4	8	9	10		3	1					12				7*		11								13
	2			5	6	4	8	9			3	1				12	10				7		11*								14
	2			5	6	4	8		10		3	1				9	11*				7		12								15
1	2			5	6	4	8		10		3					9					7		11*	12							16
1	2			5	6	4	8		10		3					12					7		11					9*			17
1				5	6	4	8		10	11	3					9					7								2		18
				5	6	4	8		10	7	3	1				12	9							11*					2		19
	2		5*	6		4	9		10	11	3	1			8	7						12									20
		11	5	6		2	8		10	4	3	1				9					7										21
		11	5	6		2	8		10	4	3	1				7	9														22
		12	11*	5	6	2	8		10	4	3	1				7	9														23
		8		5	6	2			10	4	3	1			12	7							11					9*			24
	2		11*		6	7	8		10	4	3			5	12		9														25
1	2			5	6	7	8		10*	4	3				12	11	9														26
1	2			5	6	11	8			4	3					10	9	7													27
1					6	7			10	4	3				8	11	9	2						5							28
1			9			7			10	4	3				6	11	8	2						5							29
1	11					7			10	4	3			6	5	12	8		2									9*			30
1	11						7		10	4	3			6	5		8		2	9											31
1	11						7	12	10	4	3			6	5		8*		2	9											32
1	12	11					7	9*	10	4	3			6	5		8		2												33
	12	11					7	8*	10		3		1	6	5		4		2	9											34
		11*					7		10		4		1	6	5		8			9				12	3				2		35
		12					2		10		4	3*	1	11	6	8	7			9					5						36
		11							10		4	3*	1	2	6	8	7	12		9					5						37
	3	11							10		4		1	7	6		8		2	9					5						38
	3	11							10		4		1	7	6	12	8*		2	9					5						39
	3	11				4	12		10		8		1	7*	6				2	9					5						40
	3	7					8		10		4		1		6				2	9			11		5						41
	2								10		4	3		8*	6	12	11	7	9						5					1	42
21	28	21	3	26	25	30	28	11	40	34	29	12	8	12	19	9	27	13	13	11	9	7	4	4	10	1		3	3	1	
3	2					2										11	2	3				3		2			1				
		1		5	3	9	3	6	3							2	4			1	2										

1987-88

1	Aug	15	(a)	Doncaster R	L	0-1		2,482
2		22	(h)	Gillingham	W	2-0	Walsh 2	2,901
3		29	(a)	Notts C	D	0-0		5,322
4		31	(h)	Brentford	L	0-1		3,361
5	Sep	5	(a)	Preston NE	W	3-1	Saunders, Walsh, O'Riordan	5,522
6		12	(h)	Mansfield T	L	2-3	O'Riordan, Grocock	3,410
7		15	(a)	Bury	W	2-0	McGarvey 2 (1 pen)	1,899
8		19	(a)	Chester C	L	0-1		1,897
9		26	(h)	Walsall	L	0-2		3,314
10		29	(a)	Rotherham U	D	0-0		3,375
11	Oct	3	(h)	Southend U	L	1-3	O'Riordan	2,544
12		10	(a)	Chesterfield	W	3-0	North, Walsh 2 (1 pen)	2,072
13		17	(h)	Bristol C	L	1-4	McGarvey	3,100
14		20	(h)	Blackpool	D	1-1	Turner	2,260
15		24	(a)	Northampton T	L	1-2	Turner	5,388
16		31	(h)	Brighton & HA	L	0-1		2,711
17	Nov	3	(a)	Fulham	L	0-5		3,493
18		7	(a)	Sunderland	D	1-1	North	18,197
19		21	(h)	York C	W	5-1	North 2, Robinson 2, O'Riordan	2,973
20		28	(a)	Bristol R	L	2-4	O'Riordan 2 (1 pen)	2,787
21	Dec	12	(h)	Wigan A	L	0-2		2,196
22		19	(a)	Aldershot	L	2-3	Turner, Saunders	2,405
23		26	(a)	Walsall	L	2-3	McGarvey, North	6,272
24		28	(h)	Port Vale	W	3-1	North 3	3,043
25	Jan	1	(h)	Notts C	D	0-0		5,297
26		2	(a)	Mansfield T	L	0-1		3,315
27		16	(h)	Chester C	W	2-1	McGarvey 2	2,594
28		26	(h)	Bury	W	2-0	Turner, O'Riordan	2,525
29	Feb	2	(a)	Gillingham	D	1-1	McDermott	2,993
30		6	(h)	Preston NE	L	0-1		3,790
31		13	(a)	Port Vale	L	0-2		3,417
32		20	(h)	Doncaster R	D	0-0		3,890
33		23	(a)	Brentford	W	2-0	Jobling, Saunders	3,534
34		26	(a)	Southend U	D	0-0		3,409
35	Mar	5	(a)	Bristol C	D	1-1	O'Riordan	8,343
36		8	(h)	Rotherham U	W	2-1	Cunnington, North	3,423
37		12	(h)	Chesterfield	D	1-1	Stubbs	3,464
38		19	(a)	Brighton & HA	D	0-0		7,269
39		26	(h)	Northampton T	D	2-2	Cunnington, Robinson	3,406
40	Apr	2	(h)	Sunderland	L	0-1		7,001
41		4	(a)	York C	W	2-0	Stubbs, Agnew	3,315
42		· 9	(h)	Fulham	L	0-2		3,123
43		23	(a)	Blackpool	L	0-3		2,555
44		30	(h)	Bristol R	D	0-0		2,505
45	May	2	(a)	Wigan A	W	1-0	North	2,705
46		7	(h)	Aldershot	D	1-1	North	5,639

FINAL LEAGUE POSITION: 22nd in Division Three

Appearances

Sub Appearances

Goals

Sherwood	McDermott	Agnew	Turner	Slack	Burgess	Robinson	Walsh	North	O'Riordan	McGarvey	Toale	Saunders	Dixon	Cunnington	Jobling	Watson	Curran	Grocock	Stubbs	Rawcliffe	Lever	Moore D	
1	2	3	4	5	6	7	8*	9	10	11	12												1
1	2*	3	7	5	6	4	8	9	10	11	12												2
1		3	4	5		7	8	9	10	11	2	6											3
1		3	4	5	6	7	8	9	10	11	2												4
1		3	4	5	6		8		10	11	2	7				9							5
1	12	3	4	5	6		8*	9	10	11†	2					7		14					6
1		3	4	5	6	9	12	8*	10	11	2					7							7
1		3	4	5	6	9	12	8	10	11*	2					7*		14					8
1	2	3	4	5				8	10	11	7	9*						12					9
1	2		4	5	6			8	10	11		9	3			7							10
1	2	3	4	5			12	8†	10	11	6	9				7*		14					11
1	2		4	5		6	8	9	10	11	3					7							12
1		3	4	5	6	8	9*		10	11	2					7		12					13
1		3	4	5	6	9		8	10	11	2					7*		12					14
1		3	4†	5	6	8		9	10	11	2*		14			7		12					15
1	2			5	6†	8		9	10	11		3	14			7*		4	12				16
1	2			5		4		9	10	11		8	3			6†	7	12					17
1	2			5				9	10	11		8	3			4	7*	6	12				18
1	2		4	5		6		9	10	11*		8	3				7	12					19
1	2		4			6		9	10	11	7*	8	3					5			12		20
1	2	3	4		5	6		9	10	11	7*	8					12						21
1	2*	3	4	5		6			10	11	12	8	9			7†		14					22
1		3	4	5*	6	7		9	10	11	14	8	2†					12					23
1		3	4		5	6		9	10	11		8	2				7						24
1		3	4		5	6	9*		10	11		8	2			12	7						25
1		3	4		5	6			10	11	7†	8	2			12	9*	14					26
1		3	4		5	6		9	10	11		8	2			12	7*						27
1		3	4		5	6			10	11*		8	2			12	7	9					28
1	7	3	4		5	6		9	10	11		8	2										29
1	7	3	4		5	6		9†	10	11		8	2*			14		12					30
1		3	4	5		7		9†	10		6*	8	2			12		11		14			31
1		3		5	11			9	10			8	2	4	6		7*	12					32
1	12	3		5		7		9*	10	11		8	2	4	6								33
1	9	3		5		7			10	11		8	2	4	6								34
1	14	3		5		7		9*	10	11		8†	2	4	6			12					35
1		3		5		7		9	10	11		8	2	4	6								36
1	14	3		5		7		9*	10	11		8	2†	4	6			12					37
1	14	3		5		7		9*	10	11		8†	2	4	6			12					38
1	12	3		5		7		9	10			8	2	4*	6			11					39
1	14	3		5		7		9†	10			8*	2	4	6			11	12				40
1	8	3		5		7			10				2	4	6			11	9				41
1	9	3		5		7			10		12		2*	4	6			11	8				42
1		3		5		7		9*	10	11		8	2	4	6			12					43
1		3		5		7		9	10	12		8	2	4	6			11*					44
1	9*	3		5		7		12	10	11†		8	2	4	6			14					45
1	11	3		5		7		9	10			8	2*	4	6			12					46
46	21	38	28	21	38	40	8	37	46	38	16	34	30	15	15	13	10	10	2				
	7						3	1	1	4	1	2				6	2	15	5	2	1	1	
	1	1	4			3	5	11	8	6		3		2	1			1	2				

23

1988-89

1	Aug	27	(a)	Cambridge U	L	1-4	Stoutt	2,290
2	Sep	3	(h)	Torquay U	W	1-0	North	2,889
3		10	(a)	Scunthorpe U	D	1-1	Alexander	6,037
4		17	(h)	Rotherham U	L	0-4		3,697
5		20	(a)	Wrexham	W	2-1	Jobling, North	2,267
6		24	(h)	Rochdale	L	1-3	North	2,939
7	Oct	1	(a)	Hereford U	L	1-2	O'Kelly	1,888
8		4	(h)	Tranmere R	D	0-0		2,288
9		8	(h)	Peterborough U	D	0-0		2,822
10		15	(a)	Exeter C	L	1-2	Alexander	2,232
11		22	(h)	York C	W	2-0	Cockerill, Alexander	2,829
12		25	(a)	Crewe A	D	2-2	Saunders 2	2,311
13		29	(h)	Halifax T	W	3-2	Saunders 2, O'Kelly	3,260
14	Nov	5	(a)	Stockport Co	L	1-3	McDermott	2,064
15		8	(h)	Doncaster R	W	5-0	Watson 2 (1 pen), Alexander, Saunders, Cockerill	3,382
16		12	(a)	Hartlepool U	L	1-2	Watson (pen)	1,782
17		26	(a)	Carlisle U	L	1-2	Cockerill	2,195
18	Dec	3	(h)	Scarborough	W	2-1	Alexander, Cockerill	3,887
19		17	(h)	Leyton O*	D	2-2	Lever, Saunders	3,445
20		26	(a)	Lincoln C	D	2-2	Watson, Alexander	8,038
21		31	(a)	Burnley	L	0-1		7,367
22	Jan	2	(h)	Colchester U	D	2-2	O'Kelly, Alexander	4,472
23		14	(a)	Torquay U	D	2-2	North, Alexander	2,251
24		21	(h)	Cambridge U	W	4-0	O'Kelly, Saunders, Cunnington, Tillson	3,644
25	Feb	4	(h)	Wrexham	L	0-1		5,058
26		11	(a)	Rochdale	W	2-0	Alexander 2	1,621
27		14	(h)	Darlington	D	0-0		4,628
28		25	(h)	Exeter C	W	2-1	O'Kelly, Lever	4,684
29		28	(h)	Crewe A	D	0-0		5,404
30	Mar	4	(a)	York C	W	3-0	Saunders, O'Kelly, North	3,481
31		7	(a)	Rotherham U	L	0-1		4,888
32		11	(h)	Stockport Co	W	2-0	North, Jobling	4,685
33		14	(a)	Halifax T	L	1-2	O'Kelly	1,609
34		18	(h)	Scunthorpe U	D	1-1	O'Kelly	9,796
35		24	(a)	Colchester U	D	0-0		4,507
36		27	(h)	Lincoln C	.W	1-0	O'Kelly	8,618
37	Apr	1	(a)	Leyton O	L	0-5		4,149
38		4	(a)	Darlington	D	1-1	Jobling	1,840
39		8	(h)	Burnley	W	1-0	Saunders	4,856
40		15	(h)	Hereford U	D	1-1	Gilbert	4,036
41		25	(a)	Peterborough U	W	2-1	Alexander, Jobling (pen)	2,937
42		29	(h)	Carlisle U	D	0-0		3,833
43	May	1	(a)	Doncaster R	W	3-2	Banton, Tillson, O'Kelly	2,183
44		6	(a)	Scarborough	W	3-2	Alexander 2, Saunders	3,923
45		9	(a)	Tranmere R	L	2-3	Cockerill, Gilbert	6,938
46		13	(h)	Hartlepool U	W	3-0	Cockerill, Alexander, Gilbert	3,801

FINAL LEAGUE POSITION : 9th in Division Four

Appearances

Sub Appearances

Goals

Sherwood	Dixon	Agnew	Williams	Cunnington	Cockerill	Jobling	McDermott	O'Kelly	Stoutt	North	Tillson	Reece	Lever	Alexander	Saunders	Caldwell	Grocock	Watson	Stephenson	Banton	Gilbert	Smaller	
1	2*	3	4	5	6	7	8	9	10	11	12												1
		3	4	6		7	12	9	10	8	5	1	2	11*									2
		3	4	6		7		9		8	5	1	2	11	12	10*							3
		3	4	8	6	7	12	9*			5	1		11	14	10†	2						4
	2	3	4	6		7		9		8	5	1		11				10					5
	2	3	4	6		7		9		8	5	1		11			12	10*					6
1	2*	3	4	6	14	7	10	9		8	5			11†	12								7
1		3		6		7	2	9		8	4		5	11*	10		12						8
1		3		6	7*		2	9		8	4		5	11	10		12						9
1	14	3		6	12	7*	2	9		8†	4		5	11			10						10
1		3	2*	6	10		7	9		12	4		5	11	8								11
1		3		6			2	9		7	4		5	11	8			10					12
1		3	2	6			7	9			4		5	11	8			10					13
1			2*	6	3		7	9			4		5	11	8		12	10					14
1				6	10		2	9			4		5	11	8			7	3				15
1	12			6	10		2*	9†			4		5	11	8		14	7	3				16
		3		6	10		2	9		7	4	1	5	11*	8			12					17
1		3		6	10		2	9		7	4		5	11	8								18
1		3		6	10	12	2	9*		7	4		5	11	8								19
		3			10		2	9		7*	4	1	5	11	8		12	6					20
		3			10		2	9*		7	4	1	5	11	8		12	6					21
		3		6	14	10†	2	9		12	4	1	5	11*	8			7					22
		3		6	10	7*	2			9	4	1	5	11	8			12					23
		3		6	10		2	9		7	4	1	5	11	8								24
		3		6	10	2		9		7	4	1	5*	11	8			12					25
1		3		6	10	7		9		2	4		5	11	8								26
1		3		6	10	7*		9		2	4		5	11	8			12					27
1		3		6	10		2	9		7	4		5	11	8								28
1		3		6	10		2	9		7	4		5	11*	8			12					29
1				6	10		2	9		7	4		5		8			11	3				30
1				6	10		2	9		7	4		5	12	8			11*	3				31
1				6	10		2	9		7	4		5	11	8				3				32
1				6	10		2	9		7	4		5	11	8			12	3*				33
1	12			6	10		2	9		7	4		5	11	8				3*				34
1		3		6	10	7	2	9			4		5	11	8								35
1		3		6	10	2		9			4		5	11	12					7*	8		36
1		3		6	10	7	2	9*		7			5†	11	12				14		8		37
1			5	6	10	7	2				4			11	9				3		8		38
			2	6		10					4	1	5	11	7			12	3	9*	8		39
			2	6	14	10	9*				4	1	5†	11	7				3	12	8		40
1		3	5	6	12	10	2	9*			4			11	7						8		41
1		3	5†	6	10	7*	2	12			4			11	9					14	8		42
1		3*	5	6	10		2	9			4			14	7†			12		11	8		43
1			2	6	10		9				4		5	11	7			12	3*	14	8†		44
1			2	6	10		3				4†		5	11	9			7*	14	12	8		45
1			4	6	10		2						5†	11	9			7*	3	12	8	14	46
32	4	32	19	44	24	31	36	38	2	27	44	14	37	42	36	2	4	12	12	3	11		
	1	2		5	1	2	1		2	1			2	5	1	6	9	2	5		1		
			1	6	4	1	10	1	6	2		2	14	10			4		1	3			

25

1989-90

1	Aug	19	(h)	Cambridge U	D	0-0		4,822
2		26	(a)	Torquay U	W	3-0	Childs, Cunnington, Rees	2,525
3	Sep	2	(h)	Colchester U	W	4-1	Rees 2, Watson, Daniels (og)	4,678
4		9	(a)	Carlisle U	D	1-1	Childs	3,360
5		16	(h)	Maidstone U	L	2-3	Gilbert 2 (1 pen)	5,198
6		23	(a)	York C	W	1-0	Rees	3,366
7		27	(a)	Exeter C	L	1-2	Lever	3,702
8		30	(h)	Hereford U	L	0-2		4,832
9	Oct	7	(h)	Rochdale	L	1-2	Tillson	3,996
10		14	(a)	Scarborough	L	1-3	Gilbert (pen)	2,828
11		17	(h)	Gillingham	W	2-0	Jobling, Hargreaves	3,447
12		21	(a)	Lincoln C	D	1-1	Alexander	6,251
13		28	(h)	Halifax T	D	1-1	Cunnington	4,021
14	Nov	1	(a)	Peterborough U	D	1-1	Gabbiadini	6,827
15		4	(h)	Chesterfield	L	0-1		4,513
16		11	(a)	Wrexham	W	1-0	Birtles	1,658
17		25	(h)	Aldershot	W	2-1	Agnew, Birtles	3,716
18	Dec	2	(a)	Burnley	D	1-1	Cockerill	5,615
19		19	(h)	Southend U	W	2-0	Cockerill 2 (2 pens)	4,001
20		26	(a)	Scunthorpe U	D	2-2	Alexander, Agnew	8,384
21		30	(a)	Hartlepool U	L	2-4	Rees, Alexander	3,398
22	Jan	1	(h)	Stockport Co	W	4-2	Alexander, Rees, Gilbert (pen), Birtles	5,717
23		13	(h)	Torquay U	D	0-0		4,586
24		16	(a)	Doncaster R	D	0-0		4,338
25		20	(a)	Cambridge U	L	0-2		2,623
26		27	(h)	Carlisle U	W	1-0	Alexander	4,657
27	Feb	3	(h)	York C	W	3-0	Tilson, Rees, Alexander	5,049
28		10	(a)	Maidstone U	D	2-2	Childs, Alexander	2,365
29		17	(h)	Burnley	W	4-2	Knight, Cunnington, Childs, Birtles	5,973
30		20	(a)	Colchester U	L	0-1		3,026
31		24	(a)	Aldershot	D	0-0		1,858
32	Mar	3	(h)	Doncaster R	W	2-1	Rees, Gilbert	5,536
33		7	(a)	Hereford U	W	1-0	Childs	3,013
34		10	(h)	Exeter C	W	1-0	Gilbert	6,629
35		17	(a)	Rochdale	W	1-0	Gilbert	3,058
36		20	(h)	Scarborough	W	3-0	Rees 2, Lever	7,690
37		24	(a)	Gillingham	W	2-1	Alexander, Rees	4,150
38		31	(h)	Lincoln C	W	1-0	Gilbert (pen)	11,427
39	Apr	7	(a)	Halifax T	D	2-2	Rees, Alexander	3,620
40		10	(h)	Peterborough U	L	1-2	Alexander	8,123
41		14	(a)	Stockport Co	W	4-2	Gilbert 2, Birtles, Hargreaves	4,065
42		17	(h)	Scunthorpe U	W	2-1	Tillson, Cockerill	11,894
43		20	(a)	Southend U	W	2-0	Alexander 2	4,945
44		24	(h)	Hartlepool U	D	0-0		8,687
45		28	(h)	Wrexham	W	5-1	Birtles 3, Cockerill, Rees	8,431
46	May	5	(a)	Chesterfield	L	0-2		7,501

FINAL LEAGUE POSITION : 2nd in Division Four

Appearances

Sub Appearances

Goals

Sherwood	McDermott	Agnew	Tillson	Lever	Cunnington	Childs	Gilbert	Rees	Cockerill	Alexander	Watson	Hargreaves	Williams	Reece	Birtles	Stephenson	Willis	Jobling	Smaller	Stoutt	Gabbiadini	Knight	
1	2	3	4	5	6	7	8	9†	10*	11	12	14											1
1	2*	3	4	5	6	7	8	9	10	11			12										2
	2	3	4	5	6	7	8	9		12	10			1	11*								3
	2	3	4	5	6	7	8	9	10	12				1	11*								4
	2		4	5*	6	7	8		10	11	12			1	9	3†	14						5
1	2		4	5	6	7	8	9		12	10				11*	3							6
1	2		4	5	6	7	8	9			10				11	3							7
1	2		4	5	6	7	8	9		12	10†				11	3*	14						8
1			4	5	6	7		9	10	11	2	12					8*	3					9
	2		4	5	6	7*	8	9	10†	11	14	12		1				3					10
			4	5	6			8	9		11	7	2	1				10	3				11
		3	4	5	6			8			11	7	2	1	9			10					12
	2		4	5	6	7	8			11*	10	12		1	9		14	3†					13
	2	3	4	5	6	7	8		10					1	9						11		14
	2	3		5	6	7	8	9†	10	12				1	4*		14				11		15
1	2	3	4	5	6	7	8		10						9		12			11*			16
	2	3	4	5	6	7	8		10	12		11*		1	9								17
	2	3	4	5	6	7	8		10	12		11*		1	9								18
	2	3	4	5	6	7	8	9	10	11				1									19
	2	3	4†	5	6	7	8*	9	10	11				1	12			14					20
	2		4	5	6	7	8*	9		11	14			1	12	3†		10					21
	2		4*	5	6	7	8	9		11	12			1	10			3					22
1	2		4			6	7	8	9	10	11*		12					3				5	23
1			4			6	7	8	9	10	11					3	2					5	24
1			4			6	7	8*	9	10		14	12		11	3†	2					5	25
1	2		4			6	7†	8	9	10	12				11		14	3*				5	26
1	2		4*			6	7	8	9	10	12				11			3				5	27
1	2*		4	14	6	7	8	9	10	12					11†			3				5	28
1	2		4			6	7	8	9	10	12				11*			3				5	29
1	2	14	4			6	7	8	9	10†	12				11			3				5*	30
1	2		4	5	6	7	8			10	11				9			3					31
1	2†	14	4	5*	6	7	8	9	10	12					11			3					32
1	2	12	4			6	7	8	9	10*	5				11			3					33
1	2	12	4	5	6	7	8	9	10*						11			3					34
1	2	3	4*	5	6	7	8	9		12†		14			11			10					35
1	2	3	4	5	6	7	8	9		12					11*			10					36
1		3	4	12	6*	7	8	9		5	2				11			10					37
1	2	3	4*	5		7	8	9	10						11		12	6					38
1	2	3		5		7	8*	9	10	11		12			4			6					39
1	2	3†		14	6	7	8	9*	10	11		12			5			4					40
1	2*			5	6	7	8	9†	10	11		12			4		14	3					41
1	2		4†	5	6	7*	8	9	10	14		12			11			3					42
1	2		4	5	6	7	8			10	11				9*		12	3					43
1	2		4	5	6	7†	8			10	11*		12		9		14	3					44
1	2	12	4	5	6	7	8	9	10	14					11†			3*					45
1		3†	4	5	6	7	8			11*	2	12			9			10			14		46
31	39	19	42	35	44	44	45	35	33	22	10	5	-	15	36	7	1	30	1	1	3	8	
	5		3							16	6	14	1		2	8	3				1		
		2	3	2	3	5	10	13	5	12	1	2			8			1		1	1		

1990-91

#	Month	Date		Opponent	Res	Score	Scorers	Att
1	Aug	25	(a)	Preston NE	W	3-1	Gilbert (pen), Hargreaves, Woods	6,372
2	Sep	1	(h)	Wigan A	W	4-3	Childs, Hargreaves, Woods 2	5,162
3		8	(a)	Crewe A	W	2-1	Woods, Cockerill	3,265
4		15	(h)	Bradford C	D	1-1	Oliver (og)	7,960
5		18	(h)	Huddersfield T	W	4-0	Rees, Watson, Cockerill 2	6,158
6		22	(a)	Shrewsbury T	W	2-1	Woods, Watson	2,904
7		29	(a)	Brentford	L	0-1		5,951
8	Oct	2	(h)	Rotherham U	W	2-1	Lever, Woods	6,923
9		6	(h)	Swansea C	W	1-0	Gilbert	5,974
10		13	(a)	Chester C	W	2-1	Woods, Bennett (og)	1,875
11		20	(a)	Birmingham C	D	0-0		10,123
12		23	(h)	Leyton O	D	2-2	Woods, Knight	6,660
13		27	(h)	Stoke C	W	2-0	Watson, Childs	10,799
14	Nov	3	(a)	Exeter C	D	0-0		4,647
15		10	(a)	Tranmere R	W	2-1	Cunnington, Gilbert	6,140
16		24	(h)	Bolton W	L	0-1		6,240
17	Dec	1	(h)	Mansfield T	W	2-0	Gilbert 2 (1 pen)	5,350
18		15	(a)	Southend U	L	0-2		8,126
19		22	(h)	Bournemouth	W	5-0	Rees 2, Cunnington, Gilbert 2 (1 pen)	5,651
20		26	(a)	Reading	L	0-2		3,045
21		29	(a)	Cambridge U	L	0-1		5,922
22	Jan	1	(h)	Fulham	W	3-0	Rees, Hargreaves, Childs	7,492
23		5	(h)	Bury	L	0-1		6,249
24		12	(a)	Wigan A	L	0-2		2,868
25		19	(h)	Preston NE	W	4-1	Lever, Rees 2, Childs	5,391
26		26	(a)	Bradford C	W	2-0	Watson, Gilbert	8,314
27	Feb	2	(a)	Huddersfield T	D	1-1	Watson	6,571
28		5	(h)	Shrewsbury T	W	1-0	Watson	5,683
29		16	(a)	Bolton W	D	0-0		10,318
30		23	(h)	Tranmere R	L	0-1		6,375
31	Mar	2	(a)	Mansfield T	D	1-1	Rees	3,502
32		9	(h)	Southend U	W	1-0	Gilbert	9,689
33		12	(h)	Rotherham U	W	4-1	Rees 2, Dempsey (og), Woods	5,542
34		16	(h)	Brentford	W	2-0	Woods 2	6,685
35		20	(h)	Chester C	W	2-0	Woods, Watson	6,012
36		23	(a)	Swansea C	D	0-0		3,203
37		30	(h)	Reading	W	3-0	Cockerill 2, Gilbert (pen)	7,219
38	Apr	2	(a)	Bournemouth	L	1-2	Watson	7,021
39		6	(h)	Cambridge U	W	1-0	Gilbert (pen)	8,550
40		9	(a)	Bury	L	2-3	Rees, Gilbert (pen)	4,748
41		13	(a)	Fulham	D	0-0		5,464
42		20	(h)	Birmingham C	D	0-0		8,842
43		23	(h)	Crewe A	L	0-1		7,166
44		27	(a)	Leyton O	W	2-0	Birtles, Watson	4,306
45	May	4	(a)	Stoke C	D	0-0		11,832
46		11	(h)	Exeter C	W	2-1	Cockerill 2	14,225

FINAL LEAGUE POSITION : 3rd in Division Three

Appearances

Sub Appearances

Goals

Sherwood	McDermott	Jobling	Tillson	Knight	Cunnington	Childs	Gilbert	Woods	Cockerill	Hargreaves	Rees	Watson	Alexander	Lever	Birtles	Agnew	Baraclough	Croft	Futcher	Smith	Match
1	2	3	4	5	6	7	8	9	10	11											1
1	2	3	4	5*	6	7		11	10	8†	9	12	14								2
1	2	3	4		6	7*	8	11	10		9	12		5							3
1	2	3	4		6		8	11*	10		9	7		5	12						4
1	2	3	4		6		8	11	10		9	7		5							5
1	2	3	4		6		8	11	10	9		7		5							6
1	2	3	4*	14	6		8	11	10	12	9	7		5†							7
1	2	3	4		6		8	11*	10	12	9	7		5							8
1	2	3	4		6		8	11	10		9	7		5							9
1	2	3	4		6		8	11	10		9	7		5							10
1	2	3	4		6	12	8	11	10		9	7*		5							11
1	2	3*	4	14	6	7	8	11		12	9	10		5†							12
1	2	3	4		6	7	8	11			9	10		5							13
1		3	4	14	6	7†	8	11	10	12	9*	2		5							14
1		3	4		6		8	11	10	12		7		5	9*	2					15
1	2	3	4	5	6	12	8	11	10		9†	7*			14						16
1	2	3	4	5	6	7	8	11	10		9										17
1	2*	3	4		6		8	11	10	12	9	7†		5	14						18
1	2				6	7	8	11	10		9			5	4	3					19
1	2	12			6	7†	8	11	10	9*				5	4	3	14				20
1	2	7			6	12	8	11	10*	8				5	4†	3	14				21
1	2	10			6	7		11		7	9*	12		5	4	3					22
1	2	10	14		6	7	8	11		8		12		5	4†	3*					23
1	2	3			6	7	8*	11		8		10		5	4†		14	12			24
1	2				6	7	8	11		12	9*	10		5		3			4		25
1	2	3			6	7	8	11			9	10		5					4		26
1	2	3			6	7	8*	11			9	10		5	12				4		27
1	2	3			6	7	8	11*			9	10		5	12				4		28
1	2	3			6	7	8	11*			9	10		5	12				4		29
1	2	3			6	7	8	11	14	12	9	10*		5†					4		30
1	2	3			6	7	8				9	10		5	11				4		31
1	2	3			6	7*	8	14	10		9	12		5	11†				4		32
1	2	3			6		8	12	10		9	7		5	11*				4		33
1	2	3			6		8	11	10		9	7		5					4		34
1	2	3			6		8	11	10		9	7		5					4		35
1	2	3			6		8	11	10		9	7†		5	12				4	14*	36
1	2	3			6	12	8	11†	10		9	7		5*					4	14	37
1	2	3			6		8	11†	10		9	7*		5	12				4	14	38
1	2	3			6		8		10		9	7		5					4	11	39
1	2	3			6		8	11	10		9	7†		5*	12				4	14	40
1	2	3			6		8	11	10		9*	7		5					4	12	41
1	2	3			6	12	8	11	10		9†	7*		5					4	14	42
1	2	3			6		8	11	10	12		7†		5	9				4*	14	43
1	2	3			6†		8	11*	10	12		7		5	9				4	14	44
1	2	3			6		8	11	10			7		5	9*				4	12	45
1	2	3			6		8	11	10		9*	7		5					4	12	46
46	43	44	18	4	46	20	44	42	34	8	36	36	-	40	15	6	1	-	22	1	
		1		4		5		2	1	10		5	1		8	1	3	1		10	
				1	2	4	12	12	7	3	10	9		2	1						

29

1991-92

1	Aug	17	(h)	Cambridge U	L	3-4	Watson, Rees 2		7,657
2		24	(a)	Oxford U	W	2-1	Cockerill, McDermott		4,511
3		31	(h)	Tranmere R	D	2-2	Woods 2		7,018
4	Sep	4	(a)	Leicester C	L	0-2			16,242
5		7	(a)	Bristol R	W	3-2	Jobling, Jones, Gilbert		4,641
6		14	(h)	Plymouth A	W	2-1	Jobling, Jones		5,432
7		17	(h)	Portsmouth	D	1-1	Woods		5,348
8		21	(a)	Sunderland	W	2-1	Dobbin, Cunnington		16,535
9		28	(h)	Ipswich T	L	1-2	Gilbert		6,621
10	Oct	5	(a)	Watford	L	0-2			6,930
11		12	(h)	Port Vale	L	1-2	Childs		8,218
12		19	(h)	Middlesbrough	W	1-0	Woods		10,265
13		26	(a)	Blackburn R	L	1-2	Childs		11,096
14	Nov	2	(h)	Charlton A	W	1-0	Childs		4,743
15		6	(a)	Brighton & HA	L	0-3			4,420
16		9	(a)	Newcastle U	L	0-2			16,959
17		23	(h)	Millwall	D	1-1	Cunnington		5,701
18		26	(a)	Wolves	L	1-2	Dobbin		9,378
19		30	(a)	Swindon T	D	1-1	Dobbin		8,397
20	Dec	7	(h)	Bristol C	W	3-1	Woods, Jones, Smith		4,866
21		14	(a)	Barnsley	L	1-4	Smith		6,856
22		26	(a)	Derby Co	D	0-0			16,392
23		28	(a)	Tranmere R	D	1-1	Ford		7,900
24	Jan	1	(h)	Wolves	L	0-2			9,158
25		11	(h)	Oxford U	W	1-0	Rees		5,117
26		18	(a)	Cambridge U	W	1-0	Dobbin		6,092
27	Feb	8	(h)	Blackburn R	L	2-3	Mendonca, Cunnington		10,014
28		15	(a)	Millwall	D	1-1	Rees		6,807
29		18	(h)	Southend U	W	3-2	Smith, Cunnington, Dobbin		5,337
30		22	(h)	Swindon T	D	0-0	'		6,817
31		29	(a)	Bristol C	D	1-1	Woods		8,992
32	Mar	3	(a)	Charlton A	W	3-1	Smith, Barness (og), Rees		3,658
33		7	(h)	Barnsley	L	0-1			6,913
34		10	(h)	Brighton & HA	L	0-1			4,583
35		17	(h)	Leicester C	L	0-1			6,377
36		21	(h)	Newcastle U	D	1-1	Cunnington		11,613
37		28	(a)	Southend U	L	1-3	Woods		4,591
38		31	(a)	Plymouth A	W	2-1	Mendonca, Woods		6,274
39	Apr	4	(h)	Bristol R	L	0-1			4,859
40		7	(h)	Derby Co	L	0-1			7,040
41		11	(a)	Portsmouth	L	0-2			10,576
42		18	(h)	Sunderland	W	2-0	Dobbin, Mendonca		8,864
43		21	(a)	Ipswich T	D	0-0			22,393
44		25	(h)	Watford	L	0-1			6,483
45		28	(a)	Middlesbrough	L	0-2			18,570
46	May	2	(a)	Port Vale	W	1-0	Watson		8,678

FINAL LEAGUE POSITION : 19th in Division Two

Appearances

Sub Appearances

Goals

Sherwood	McDermott	Jobling	Futcher	Lever	Dobbin	Watson	Gilbert	Rees	Smith	Woods	Jones	Agnew	Cockerill	Birtles	North	Childs	Cunnington	Hargreaves	Reece	Ford	Rodger	Mendonca	Knight	#
1	2	3	4	5	6†	7	8	9	10*	11	12	14												1
1	2	3	4	5	6	7	8		14	11†	9*		10	12										2
1	2	3	4	5	6	7†	8		14	11	9*		10	12										3
1	2	3	4	5	6	7	8		14	11	9*		10†	12										4
1	2	3	4	5	6	7†	8		14	11	9*	10		12										5
1	2	3	4	5	6	7†	8		14	11*	9	10			12									6
1	2	3	4	5	6		8		12	11	9	10				7*								7
1	2		4	5	10		8		11		9	3				7*	6	12						8
1	2	4*		5	10		8	14	3	11	9†					7	6	12						9
1	2		4	5	10†		8	9	3	11	14			12		7*	6							10
1	2*		4		10†	12	8	9	3	11	14		5			7	6							11
1	2	3	4	5		10	8	9		11						7	6							12
1	2	3	4	5		10†	8	9		11	12	14				7*	6							13
1	2			5	14		8*	12		11	3	10†	4			7	6	9						14
1	2		4	5			8*			11	12	3	10			7	6	9						15
1	2*			5	10		8			11	9	3	12	4		7	6							16
		3	4		10			9	8	11*	12	5				7	6			1	2			17
		3	4		8			9	12	11		5	10			7	6*			1	2			18
		3	4		6	8*		9	12	11		5	10			7				1	2			19
		3	4		6		8	9		11	12	5	10*			7				1	2			20
		3	4†	14	10		8	9		11	12	5				7*	6			1	2			21
	2	10	4	5			8			11	9	3					6			1	7			22
	2		4	5	6		8		10		9	3				11		12	1*	7				23
1	2		4†	5	6	14	8	9	3	10*						11		12		7				24
	2	3		5	6		8	9*		12						7			1	11	4	10		25
	2	3		5	6		8	9		12						7			1	11	4	10*		26
	2†	3		5	11		8	9		12						7*	6		1	14	4	10		27
	2	3		5	11		8*	9	10		12					7	6		1		4			28
	2	3		5	11		8*	9	10		12					7†	6		1	14	4			29
	2	3		5	11		8	9	10*		12					7	6		1		4			30
	2	3		5	11†		8	9	10		12	14				7*	6		1				4	31
	2	3		5	11*		8	9	10			12				7	6		1				4	32
	2	3	5*		11		8	9	10		12					7	6		1				4	33
	2			5	11		8	9	10		12		3			7*	6		1	14			4†	34
	2	3	5†		8	9*			10	11						7	6	12	1	14	4			35
	2	3	4	5	9		8*			11	12						6		1	7		10		36
1	2	3	4*	5	9†		8			11	12	14					6			7		10		37
1	2			5			8	9		11		3					6			7	4	10		38
1	2	14		5			8	9*		11	12	3†					6			7	4	10		39
1	2	3		5			8†		12	11	9						6	14		7*	4	10		40
	2			5	12		8	3		11	9*						6	14	1	7	4	10†		41
	2	3	5	9			8			11						7*	6		1	12	4	10		42
	2	3	5		7		8	9		11		10					6		1		4			43
	2	3	5		7	8*		9		11†	12						6	14	1	10	4			44
	2	3	5		7	8		9*	12	11		10					6		1		4			45
	2	3	5		7	8		9*		11	12	10					6		1		4			46
21	39	35	29	35	32	13	41	22	28	30	14	20	8	3	-	29	33	2	25	17	16	10	4	
	1		1		4	1		12	7	14	4		2	5	1		8		5		.			
	1	2			6	2	2	5	4	8	3		1			3	5			1		3		

1992-93

1	Aug	15	(a)	Charlton A	L	1-3	Dobbin	4,823
2		22	(h)	Watford	W	3-2	Mendonca, Watson, Rodger	4,772
3		30	(a)	Birmingham C	L	1-2	Mendonca	6,807
4	Sep	5	(h)	Oxford U	D	1-1	Mendonca (pen)	4,546
5		12	(a)	Tranmere R	D	1-1	Watson	5,330
6		19	(a)	Bristol R	W	3-0	Rees, Woods	5,320
7		26	(h)	Cambridge U	D	1-1	Rodger	4,848
8		29	(a)	Swindon T	L	0-1		5,759
9	Oct	3	(h)	Peterborough U	L	1-3	Rodger	5,208
10		10	(a)	Notts Co	L	0-1		6,442
11		17	(h)	Southend U	W	1-0	Rodger	4,117
12		24	(a)	Newcastle U	W	1-0	Dobbin	30,088
13		31	(h)	Portsmouth	W	3-0	Gilbert, McDermott, Rees	5,708
14	Nov	3	(h)	West Ham U	D	1-1	Mendonca	9,119
15		7	(a)	Luton T	W	4-1	Groves 3, Rees	6,928
16		14	(h)	Bristol C	W	2-1	Watson, Mendonca	5,651
17		21	(a)	Brentford	W	3-1	Mendonca, Groves, Dobbin	7,439
18		28	(a)	Wolverhampton W	L	1-2	Lever	14,240
19	Dec	5	(h)	Leicester C	L	1-3	Groves	7,408
20		12	(a)	Millwall	L	1-2	McDermott	6,900
21		20	(h)	Derby Co	L	0-2		6,475
22		26	(h)	Barnsley	W	4-2	Gilbert 2, Groves, Watson	8,242
23		28	(a)	Sunderland	L	0-2		20,771
24	Jan	9	(h)	Bristol R	W	2-0	Dobbin, Rees	4,922
25		16	(a)	Cambridge U	L	0-2		4,137
26		26	(h)	Swindon T	W	2-1	Rees, Groves	5,207
27		30	(a)	Watford	W	3-2	Rodger, Mendonca, Groves	6,613
28	Feb	6	(h)	Charlton A	W	1-0	Rodger	5,403
29		20	(h)	Birmingham C	D	1-1	Rodger	5,237
30		23	(a)	Oxford U	W	1-0	Gilbert	4,944
31		27	(h)	Notts Co	D	3-3	Groves 3	5,871
32	Mar	6	(a)	Peterborough U	L	0-1		6,657
33		9	(a)	West Ham U	L	1-2	Groves	13,170
34		13	(h)	Luton T	W	3-1	Ford 2, Mendonca	5,193
35		16	(h)	Tranmere R	D	0-0		5,686
36		20	(a)	Leicester C	L	0-3		15,930
37		23	(h)	Brentford	L	0-1		4,384
38		27	(a)	Bristol C	L	0-1		6,755
39	Apr	3	(h)	Wolverhampton W	W	1-0	Agnew	5,080
40		6	(h)	Millwall	W	1-0	Mendonca	4,445
41		10	(a)	Barnsley	W	2-0	Dobbin, Mendonca	4,958
42		12	(h)	Sunderland	W	1-0	Woods	8,090
43		17	(a)	Derby Co	L	1-2	Woods	12,428
44		.23	(a)	Southend U	L	0-1		5,807
45	May	4	(h)	Newcastle U	L	0-2		14,402
46		8	(a)	Portsmouth	L	1-2	Daws	24,955

FINAL LEAGUE POSITION: 9th in Division One

Appearances

Sub Appearances

Goals

32

Wilmot	McDermott	Jobling	Baraclough	Rodger	Dobbin	Watson	Gilbert	Rees	Mendonca	Woods	Smith	Groves	Agnew	Ford	Handyside	Hargreaves	Futcher	Croft	Childs	Tillson	Lever	Beasant	Sherwood	Daws						
1	2	3	4	5	6	7	8	9*	10	11†	12	14																		1
1	2	3		5	6	7	8		10	11		9	4																	2
1	2	3			6	7			10	11	8*	9	5		4	12														3
1	2*	3			6	7		12	10	11		9	5	8	4															4
1		3		4	6	7	8	12	10	11*		9			5			2												5
1				5	6	7	8	9		11		10					2	3		4										6
1	2			5	6	7	8		9†	11	14	10*						3	12	4										7
1				5	6	7*	8		9	11†	14	10					2	3	12	4										8
1		3†		5	6	7	8		9	11	12	10						2*	12	4										9
1				4	6	2		9	12	11*	14	10					8†	3	7		5									10
1	2			4	6		8	9*	12	11		10						3	7		5									11
	2				6	7	8		10	11		9					4	3			5	1								12
	2				6	7	8	12	10	11*		9					4	3			5	1								13
	2				6	7	8	11*	10		12	9					4	3			5	1								14
	2			12	6†	7	8	11	10		14	9					4	3			5*	1								15
	2			12	6	7	8	11	10	14		9					4†	3			5*	1								16
	2				6	7	8	11†	10	14		9					4	3			5	1								17
1	2			12	6	7	8	11*	10	14		9					4†	3			5									18
1	2			4		6	8	11	10†		12	9				14		3	7*		5									19
1	2			5	6	7*	8†			11	10	9	12			14	4	3												20
	2			5	6	7	8	9		11†	12	10				14	4*	3					1							21
	2			4	6	7	8	11	10*	12		9	3		5								1							22
	2			4	6	7	8	11	10*	12	14	9	3		5†								1							23
1	2			5	6	7*	8	11	10*		12	9	3				4†													24
1	2			5	6	7*	8	11			10	9	3	14			4†	12												25
1	2			5	6		8	11*	10		12	9	3				4		7											26
1	2			5	6			11	10		8	9	3	14			4		7†											27
1	2			4	6			11	10		8	9	3				4		7											28
	2	14		5	6		8	11*	10		12	9	3				4		7†				1							29
	2			5	6		8		10		11	9	3				4		7				1							30
		14		5	6		8	12	10		11*	9	3				4†	2	7				1							31
	2			5†	6		8	12	10		11	9	3				4	14	7*				1							32
1	2	6					8†	10	12	11*		9	14	7			4	3			5									33
1	2	6					8	11	10			9		7			4	3			5									34
1	2	6					8	11	10			9		7			4	3			5									35
1	2	6*					8	11†	10			9	14	7			4	3	12		5									36
1	2	6†		5			8		10	11*	12	9	3	7			4	14												37
1				5			8	11	10*	12		9	3	6			4	2†	7					14						38
1					6		8		14	11†		10	3	7	5		4	2						9						39
1	2				6		8		10			11	3	7	5		4							9						40
1	2				6		8	12	10†	14		11	3	7	5		4							9*						41
1	2				6		8	12	10	14		11		7	5†		4	3						9*						42
1	2				6		8		10	9	14	11	3*	7	5†		4	12												43
1	2	12			6		8†		10	9	14	11		7	5*		4	3												44
1	2			5	6		8†		10	11	14	9		7			4*	3	12											45
1	2			5	6		8†		10*	12	14	11		7			4	3						9						46
33	38	11	1	27	39	24	41	24	38	21	8	45	20	15	11	-	35	28	11	4	14	6	7	5						
		3		3				7	4	9	18	1	3	2		4		4	5					1						
	2			7	5	4	4	5	10	3		12	1	2							1			1						

F.A. CUP COMPETITION

1983/84 SEASON
3rd Round
Jan 7 vs Portsmouth (a) 1-2
Att: 12,707   Drinkell

1984/85 SEASON
3rd Round
Jan 5 vs Notts County (a) 2-2
Att: 6,202   Ford, Lund

Replay
Jan 8 vs Notts County (h) 4-2
Att: 6,743   Wilkinson, Lund 3

4th Round
Jan 26 vs Watford (h) 1-3
Att: 12,989   Foley

1985/86 SEASON
3rd Round
Jan 4 vs Arsenal (h) 3-4
Att: 12,829   Lund, Lyons, Peake (pen)

1986/87 SEASON
3rd Round
Jan 10 vs Stoke City (h) 1-1
Att: 7,367   Walsh

Replay
Jan 26 vs Stoke City (a) 1-1
Att: 14,340   Moore

2nd Replay
Jan 28 vs Stoke City (a) 0-6
Att: 12,087

1987/88 SEASON
1st Round
Nov 14 vs Scarborough (a) 2-1
Att: 3,764   McGarvey, North

2nd Round
Dec 5 vs Halifax Town (h) 0-0
Att: 3,239

Replay
Dec 8 vs Halifax Town (a) 0-2
Att: 2,633

1988/89 SEASON
1st Round
Nov 19 vs Wolverhampton Wanderers (h) 1-0
Att: 7,922   Cockerill

2nd Round
Dec 10 vs Rotherham United (h) 3-2
Att: 5,676   North, Cunnington, Russell (og)

3rd Round
Jan 7 vs Middlesbrough (a) 2-1
Att: 19,190   North 2

4th Round
Jan 28 vs Reading (h) 1-1
Att: 9,401   North

Replay
Feb 1 vs Reading (a) 2-1
Att: 8,541   Cunnington, Jobling

5th Round
Feb 18 vs Wimbledon (a) 1-3
Att: 12,517   Alexander

1989/90 SEASON
1st Round
Nov 17 vs York City (a) 2-1
Att: 4,128   Hargreaves 2

2nd Round
Dec 9 vs Doncaster Rovers (h) 1-0
Att: 6,623   Cockerill

3rd Round
Jan 6 vs Huddersfield Town (a) 1-3
Att: 9,901   Gilbert

1990/91 SEASON
1st Round
Nov 17 vs Blackpool (a) 0-2
Att: 4,175

1991/92 SEASON
1st Round
Nov 15 vs Blackpool (a) 1-2
Att: 4,074   Cunnington

1992/93 SEASON
3rd Round
Jan 2 vs Brentford (a) 2-0
Att: 6,880   Mendonca, Dobbin

4th Round
Feb 2 vs Swansea City (a) 0-0
Att: 8,307

Replay
Feb 9 vs Swansea City (h) 2-0
Att: 8,452   Mendonca, Gilbert

5th Round
Feb 13 vs Ipswich Town (a) 0-4
Att: 17,894

LEAGUE CUP COMPETITION

1983/84 SEASON
1st Round (1st leg)
Aug 30 vs York City (a) 1-2
Att: 3,505   Wilkinson

1st Round (2nd leg)
Sep 13 vs York City (h) 2-0 (aggregate 3-2)
Att: 3,529   Drinkell 2

2nd Round (1st leg)
Oct 4 vs Coventry City (h) 0-0
Att: 6,088

2nd Round (2nd leg)
Oct 25 vs Coventry City (a) 1-2 (aggregate 1-2)
Att: 8,705   Wilkinson

1984/85 SEASON
2nd Round (1st leg)
Sep 25 vs Barnsley (h) 3-0
Att: 3,577   K.Moore, Wilkinson, Bonnyman (pen)

2nd Round (2nd leg)
Oct 9 vs Barnsley (a) 1-1 (aggregate 4-1)
Att: 5,578   Foley

3rd Round
Oct 30 vs Rotherham United (a) 0-0
Att: 8,413

Replay
Nov 6 vs Rotherham United (h) 6-1
Att: 7,649   Foley, Ford, Wilkinson, Lund, Bonnyman, Emson

4th Round
Nov 20 vs Everton (a) 1-0
Att: 26,298   Wilkinson

5th Round
Jan 16 vs Norwich City (h) 0-1
Att: 15,050

1985/86 SEASON
2nd Round (1st leg)
Sep 24 vs York City (h) 1-1
Att: 2,908   Gilligan

2nd Round (2nd leg)
Oct 8 vs York City (a) 3-2 (aggregate 4-3)
Att: 5,030   Hobson 2, Gilligan

3rd Round
Oct 29 vs Ipswich Town (h) 0-2
Att: 6,684

1986/87 SEASON
1st Round (1st leg)
Sep 2 vs Carlisle United (a) 0-1
Att: 2,861

1st Round (2nd leg)
Sep 9 vs Carlisle United (h) 2-0 (aggregate 2-1)
Att: 3,902   Walsh 2

2nd Round (1st leg)
Sep 23 vs Hull City (a) 0-1
Att: 5,115

2nd Round (2nd leg)
Oct 7 vs Hull City (h) 1-1 (aggregate 1-2)
Att: 5,471   Walsh

1987/88 SEASON
1st Round (1st leg)
Aug 18 vs Darlington (h) 3-2
Att: 2,248   Walsh, McGarvey, North

1st Round (2nd leg)
Aug 26 vs Darlington (a) 1-2 (aet) (agg. 4-4)
Att: 1,237   North   Darlington win on away goals

1988/89 SEASON
1st Round (1st leg)
Aug 30 vs Rotherham United (h) 0-1
Att: 2,517

1st Round (2nd leg)
Sep 6 vs Rotherham United (a) 0-1 (agg. 0-2)
Att: 3,381

1989/90 SEASON
1st Round (1st leg)
Aug 22 vs Hull City (a) 0-1
Att: 5,045

1st Round (2nd leg)
Aug 28 vs Hull City (h) 2-0 (aggregate 2-1)
Att: 6,758   Alexander, Childs

2nd Round (1st leg)
Sep 19 vs Coventry City (h) 3-1
Att: 10,150   Gilbert, Watson, Birtles

2nd Round (2nd leg)
Oct 4 vs Coventry City (a) 0-3 (aggregate 3-4)
Att: 15,327

1990/91 SEASON
1st Round (1st leg)
Aug 28 vs Crewe Alexandra (h) 2-1
Att: 3,882   Gilbert, Hargreaves

1st Round (2nd leg)
Sep 3 vs Crewe Alexandra (a) 0-1 (aggregate 2-2)
Att: 2,781   Crewe go through on away goals

1991/92 SEASON
1st Round (1st leg)
Aug 20 vs Rotherham United (a) 3-1
Att: 3,839   Dobbin, Jones, Rees

1st Round (2nd leg)
Aug 27 vs Rotherham United (h) 1-0 (agg. 4-1)
Att: 3,637   Birtles

2nd Round (1st leg)
Sep 25 vs Aston Villa (h) 0-0
Att: 13,835

2nd Round (2nd leg)
Oct 9 vs Aston Villa (a) 1-1 (aet) (aggregate 1-1)
Att: 15,338   Gilbert (pen)
Grimsby go through on the away goals rule

3rd Round
Oct 29 vs Tottenham Hotspur (h) 0-3
Att: 17,017

1992/93 SEASON
1st Round (1st leg)
Aug 19 vs Barnsley (h) 1-1
Att: 3,927   Mendonca

1st Round (2nd leg)
Aug 25 vs Barnsley (a) 1-1 (aet.) (aggregate 2-2)
Att: 4,636   Mendonca
Grimsby win 5-3 on penalties

2nd Round (1st leg)
Sep 28 vs QPR (a) 1-2
Att: 7,275   Watson

2nd Round (2nd leg)
Oct 6 vs QPR (h) 2-1 (aet.) (aggregate 3-3)
Att: 8,443   Sinton (og), Woods
QPR win 6-5 on penalties

1983-84 SEASON

SECOND DIVISION

Chelsea	42	25	13	4	90	40	89
Sheffield Wednesday	42	26	10	6	72	34	89
Newcastle United	42	24	8	10	85	53	80
Manchester City	42	20	10	12	66	48	70
Grimsby Town	**42**	**19**	**13**	**10**	**60**	**47**	**70**
Blackburn Rovers	42	17	16	9	57	46	67
Carlisle United	42	16	16	10	48	41	64
Shrewsbury Town	42	17	10	15	49	53	61
Brighton & Hove Alb.	42	17	9	16	69	60	60
Leeds United	42	16	12	14	55	56	60
Fulham	42	15	12	15	60	53	57
Huddersfield Town	42	14	15	13	56	49	57
Charlton Athletic	42	16	9	17	53	64	57
Barnsley	42	15	7	20	57	53	52
Cardiff City	42	15	6	21	53	66	51
Portsmouth	42	14	7	21	73	64	49
Middlesbrough	42	12	13	17	41	47	49
Crystal Palace	42	12	11	19	42	52	47
Oldham Athletic	42	13	8	21	47	73	47
Derby County	42	11	9	22	36	72	42
Swansea City	42	7	8	27	36	85	29
Cambridge United	42	4	12	26	28	77	24

1984-85 SEASON

SECOND DIVISION

Oxford United	42	25	9	8	84	36	84
Birmingham City	42	25	7	10	59	33	82
Manchester City	42	21	11	10	66	40	74
Portsmouth	42	20	14	8	69	50	74
Blackburn Rovers	42	21	10	11	66	41	73
Brighton & Hove Alb.	42	20	12	10	58	34	72
Leeds United	42	19	12	11	66	43	69
Shrewsbury Town	42	18	11	13	66	53	65
Fulham	42	19	8	15	68	64	65
Grimsby Town	**42**	**18**	**8**	**16**	**72**	**64**	**62**
Barnsley	42	14	16	12	42	42	58
Wimbledon	42	16	10	16	71	75	58
Huddersfield Town	42	15	10	17	52	64	55
Oldham Athletic	42	15	8	19	49	67	53
Crystal Palace	42	12	12	18	46	65	48
Carlisle United	42	13	8	21	50	67	47
Charlton Athletic	42	11	12	19	51	63	45
Sheffield United	42	10	14	18	54	66	44
Middlesbrough	42	10	10	22	41	57	40
Notts County	42	10	7	25	45	73	37
Cardiff	42	9	8	25	47	79	35
Wolves	42	8	9	25	37	79	33

1985-86 SEASON

SECOND DIVISION

Norwich City	42	25	9	8	84	39	84
Charlton Athletic	42	22	11	9	78	45	77
Wimbledon	42	21	13	8	58	37	76
Portsmouth	42	22	7	13	69	41	73
Crystal Palace	42	19	9	14	57	52	66
Hull City	42	17	13	12	65	55	64
Sheffield United	42	17	11	14	64	63	62
Oldham Athletic	42	17	9	16	62	61	60
Millwall	42	17	8	17	64	65	59
Stoke City	42	14	15	13	48	50	57
Brighton & Hove Alb.	42	16	8	18	64	64	56
Barnsley	42	14	14	14	47	50	56
Bradford City	42	16	6	20	51	63	54
Leeds United	42	15	8	19	56	72	53
Grimsby Town	**42**	**14**	**10**	**18**	**58**	**62**	**52**
Huddersfield Town	42	14	10	18	51	67	52
Shrewsbury Town	42	14	9	19	52	64	51
Sunderland	42	13	11	18	47	61	50
Blackburn Rovers	42	12	13	17	53	62	49
Carlisle United	42	13	7	22	47	71	46
Middlesbrough	42	12	9	21	44	53	45
Fulham	42	10	6	26	45	69	36

1986-87 SEASON

SECOND DIVISION

Derby County	42	25	9	8	64	38	84
Portsmouth	42	23	9	10	53	28	78
Oldham Athletic	42	22	9	11	65	44	75
Leeds United	42	19	11	12	58	44	68
Ipswich Town	42	17	13	12	59	43	64
Crystal Palace	42	19	5	18	51	53	62
Plymouth Argyle	42	16	13	13	62	57	61
Stoke City	42	16	10	16	63	53	58
Sheffield United	42	15	13	14	50	49	58
Bradford City	42	15	10	17	62	62	55
Barnsley	42	14	13	15	49	52	55
Blackburn Rovers	42	15	10	17	45	55	55
Reading	42	14	11	17	52	59	53
Hull City	42	13	14	15	41	55	53
West Brom	42	13	12	17	51	49	51
Millwall	42	14	9	19	39	45	51
Huddersfield Town	42	13	12	17	54	61	51
Shrewsbury Town	42	15	6	21	41	63	51
Birmingham City	42	11	17	14	47	59	50
Sunderland	42	12	12	18	49	59	48
Grimsby Town	**42**	**10**	**14**	**18**	**39**	**59**	**44**
Brighton & Hove Alb.	42	9	12	21	37	54	39

1987-88 SEASON
THIRD DIVISION

Sunderland	46	27	12	7	92	48	93
Brighton & Hove Alb.	46	23	15	8	69	47	84
Walsall	46	23	13	10	68	50	82
Notts County	46	23	12	11	82	49	81
Bristol City	46	21	12	13	77	62	75
Northampton Town	46	18	19	9	70	51	73
Wigan Athletic	46	20	12	14	70	61	72
Bristol Rovers	46	18	12	16	68	56	66
Fulham	46	19	9	18	69	60	66
Blackpool	46	17	14	15	71	62	65
Port Vale	46	18	11	17	58	56	65
Brentford	46	16	14	16	53	59	62
Gillingham	46	14	17	15	77	61	59
Bury	46	15	14	17	58	57	59
Chester City	46	14	16	16	51	62	58
Preston North End	46	15	13	18	48	59	58
Southend United	46	14	13	19	65	83	55
Chesterfield	46	15	10	21	41	70	55
Mansfield Town	46	14	12	20	48	59	54
Aldershot	46	15	8	23	64	74	53
Rotherham United	46	12	16	18	50	66	52
Grimsby Town	**46**	**12**	**14**	**20**	**48**	**58**	**50**
York City	46	8	9	29	48	91	33
Doncaster Rovers	46	8	9	29	40	84	33

1988-89 SEASON
FOURTH DIVISION

Rotherham United	46	22	16	8	76	35	82
Tranmere Rovers	46	21	17	8	62	43	80
Crewe Alexandra	46	21	15	10	67	48	78
Scunthorpe United	46	21	14	11	77	57	77
Scarborough	46	21	14	11	67	52	77
Leyton Orient	46	21	12	13	86	50	75
Wrexham	46	19	14	13	77	63	71
Cambridge United	46	18	14	14	71	62	68
Grimsby Town	**46**	**17**	**15**	**14**	**65**	**59**	**66**
Lincoln City	46	18	10	18	64	60	64
York City	46	17	13	16	62	63	64
Carlisle United	46	15	15	16	53	52	60
Exeter City	46	18	6	22	65	68	60
Torquay United	46	17	8	21	45	60	59
Hereford United	46	14	16	16	66	72	58
Burnley	46	14	13	19	52	61	55
Peterborough United	46	14	12	20	52	74	54
Rochdale	46	13	14	19	56	82	53
Hartlepool United	46	14	10	22	50	78	52
Stockport County	46	10	21	15	54	52	51
Halifax Town	46	13	11	22	69	75	50
Colchester United	46	12	14	20	60	78	50
Doncaster Rovers	46	13	10	23	49	78	49
Darlington	46	8	18	20	53	76	42

1989-90 SEASON
FOURTH DIVISION

Exeter City	46	28	5	13	83	48	89
Grimsby Town	**46**	**22**	**13**	**11**	**70**	**47**	**79**
Southend United	46	22	9	15	61	48	75
Stockport County	46	21	11	14	67	61	74
Maidstone United	46	22	7	17	77	61	73
Cambridge United	46	21	10	15	76	66	73
Chesterfield	46	19	14	13	63	50	71
Carlisle United	46	21	8	17	61	60	71
Peterborough United	46	17	17	12	59	46	68
Lincoln City	46	18	14	14	48	48	68
Scunthorpe United	46	17	15	14	69	54	66
Rochdale	46	20	6	20	51	54	66
York City	46	16	16	14	55	53	64
Gillingham	46	17	11	18	46	48	62
Torquay United	46	15	12	19	53	66	57
Burnley	46	14	14	18	45	55	56
Hereford United	46	15	10	21	56	62	55
Scarborough	46	15	10	21	60	73	55
Hartlepool United	46	15	10	21	66	88	55
Doncaster Rovers	46	14	9	23	53	60	51
Wrexham	46	13	12	21	51	67	51
Aldershot	46	12	14	20	49	69	50
Halifax Town	46	12	13	21	57	65	49
Colchester United	46	11	10	25	48	75	43

1990-91 SEASON
THIRD DIVISION

Cambridge United	46	25	11	10	75	45	86
Southend United	46	26	7	13	77	51	85
Grimsby Town	**46**	**24**	**11**	**11**	**66**	**44**	**83**
Bolton Wanderers	46	24	11	11	64	50	83
Tranmere Rovers	46	23	9	14	64	46	78
Brentford	46	21	13	12	59	47	76
Bury	46	20	13	13	67	56	73
Bradford City	46	20	10	16	62	54	70
Bournemouth	46	19	13	14	58	58	70
Wigan Athletic	46	20	9	17	71	54	69
Huddersfield Town	46	18	13	15	57	51	67
Birmingham City	46	16	17	13	45	49	65
Leyton Orient	46	18	10	18	55	58	64
Stoke City	46	16	12	18	55	59	60
Reading	46	17	8	21	53	66	59
Exeter City	46	16	9	21	58	52	57
Preston North End	46	15	11	20	54	67	56
Shrewsbury Town	46	14	10	22	61	68	52
Chester City	46	14	9	23	46	58	51
Swansea City	46	13	9	24	49	72	48
Fulham	46	10	16	20	41	56	46
Crewe Alexandra	46	11	11	24	62	80	44
Rotherham United	46	10	12	24	50	87	42
Mansfield Town	46	8	14	24	42	63	38

1991-92 SEASON

SECOND DIVISION

Ipswich Town	46	24	12	10	70	50	84
Middlesbrough	46	23	11	12	58	41	80
Derby County	46	23	9	14	69	51	78
Leicester City	46	23	8	15	62	55	77
Cambridge United	46	19	17	10	65	47	74
Blackburn Rvrs	46	21	11	14	70	53	74
Charlton Athletic	46	20	11	15	54	48	71
Swindon Town	46	18	15	13	69	55	69
Portsmouth	46	19	12	15	65	51	69
Watford	46	18	11	17	51	48	65
Wolves	46	18	10	18	61	54	64
Southend United	46	17	11	18	63	63	62
Bristol Rovers	46	16	14	16	60	63	62
Tranmere Rovers	46	14	19	13	56	56	61
Millwall	46	17	10	19	64	71	61
Barnsley	46	16	11	19	46	57	59
Bristol City	46	13	15	18	55	71	54
Sunderland	46	14	11	21	61	65	53
Grimsby Town	**46**	**14**	**11**	**21**	**47**	**62**	**53**
Newcastle United	46	13	13	20	66	84	52
Oxford United	46	13	11	22	66	73	50
Plymouth Argyle	46	13	9	24	42	64	48
Brighton & Hove Alb.	46	12	11	23	56	77	47
Port Vale	46	10	15	21	42	59	45

1992-93 SEASON

FIRST DIVISION

Newcastle United	46	29	9	8	92	38	96
West Ham United	46	26	10	10	81	41	88
Portsmouth	46	26	10	10	80	46	88
Tranmere Rovers	46	23	10	13	72	56	79
Swindon Town	46	21	13	12	74	59	76
Leicester City	46	22	10	14	71	64	76
Millwall	46	18	16	12	65	53	70
Derby County	46	19	9	18	68	57	66
Grimsby Town	**46**	**19**	**7**	**20**	**58**	**57**	**64**
Peterborough United	46	16	14	16	55	63	62
Wolves	46	16	13	17	57	56	61
Charlton Athletic	46	16	13	17	49	46	61
Barnsley	46	17	9	20	56	60	60
Oxford United	46	14	14	18	53	56	56
Bristol City	46	14	14	18	49	67	56
Watford	46	14	13	19	57	71	55
Notts County	46	12	16	18	55	70	52
Southend United	46	13	13	20	54	64	52
Birmingham City	46	13	12	21	50	72	51
Luton Town	46	10	21	15	48	62	51
Sunderland	46	13	11	22	50	64	50
Brentford	46	13	10	23	52	71	49
Cambridge United	46	11	16	19	48	69	49
Bristol Rovers	46	10	11	25	55	87	41

Bob Cumming. One of Grimsby's most popular players who finally left the club in 1987 after 14 years' service

AGNEW, Paul

Lisburn, 15th August 1965

From Cliftonville

Source	Season	Club	Apps	Gls
	1983-84	Grimsby T	1	-
	1984-85		12	-
	1985-86		16	-
	1986-87		29	-
	1987-88		38	1
	1988-89		34	-
	1989-90		24	2
	1990-91		7	-
	1991-92		24	-
	1992-93		23	1

ALEXANDER, Keith

Nottingham, 14th November 1958

Source	Season	Club	Apps	Gls
Barnet	1988-89	Grimsby T	44	14
	1989-90		38	12
	1990-91		1	-
Tr	1990-91	Stockport Co	11	-
Tr	1990-91	Lincoln C	23	3
	1991-92		15	1
	1992-93		7	-

BANTON, Dale C.

Kensington, 15th April 1961

Source	Season	Club	Apps	Gls
App	1979-80	West Ham U	4	-
	1981-82		1	-
Tr	1982-83	Aldershot	45	24
	1983-84		46	19
	1984-85		15	4
Tr	1984-85	York C	30	12
	1985-86		35	10
	1986-87		29	6
	1987-88		33	16
	1988-89		11	4
Tr	1988-89	Walsall	10	-
Tr	1988-89	Grimsby T	8	1
Tr	1989-90	Aldershot	23	1
	1990-91		21	2

BARACLOUGH, Ian R.

Leicester, 4th December 1970

Source	Season	Club	Apps	Gls
YT	1988-89	Leicester C	-	-
L	1989-90	Wigan A	9	2
L	1990-91	Grimsby T	4	-
Tr	1991-92		-	-
	1992-93		1	-
Tr	1992-93	Lincoln C	36	-

BARRATT, Anthony

Salford, 18th October 1965

From Billingham Town

Source	Season	Club	Apps	Gls
	1985-86	Grimsby T	22	-
Tr	1986-87	Hartlepool U	23	-
	1987-88		43	3

Source	Season	Club	Apps	Gls
	1988-89		32	1
Tr	1988-89	York C	12	-
	1989-90		46	4
	1990-91		29	1
	1991-92		21	3
	1992-93		10	-

BATCH, Nigel A.

Huddersfield, 9th November 1957

Source	Season	Club	Apps	Gls
App		Derby Co	-	-
Tr	1976-77	Grimsby T	8	-
	1977-78		10	-
	1978-79		46	-
	1979-80		46	-
	1980-81		42	-
	1981-82		42	-
	1982-83		38	-
	1983-84		42	-
	1984-85		23	-
	1985-86		30	-
	1986-87		21	-
Tr	1987-88	Lincoln C	32	-
Tr	1988-89	Darlington	30	-
L	1989-90	Stockport Co	12	-
(Local)	1991-92	Scunthorpe U	1	-

BEASANT, Dave

Willesden, 20th March 1959

From Edgware Town

Source	Season	Club	Apps	Gls
	1979-80	Wimbledon	2	-
	1980-81		34	-
	1981-82		46	-
	1982-83		46	-
	1983-84		46	-
	1984-85		42	-
	1985-86		42	-
	1986-87		42	-
	1987-88		40	-
Tr	1988-89	Newcastle U	20	-
Tr	1988-89	Chelsea	22	-
	1989-90		38	-
	1990-91		35	-
	1991-92		21	-
	1992-93		17	-
L	1992-93	Grimsby T	6	-
L	1992-93	Wolverhampton W	4	-

BIRTLES, Garry

Nottingham, 27th July 1956

From Long Eaton United

Source	Season	Club	Apps	Gls
	1976-78	Nottingham F	1	-
	1978-79		35	14
	1979-80		42	12
	1980-81		9	6
Tr	1980-81	Manchester U	25	-
	1981-82		33	-
Tr	1982-83	Nottingham F	25	7
	1983-84		34	15
	1984-85		13	2

Source	Season	Club	Apps.	Gls
	1985-86	Nottingham F	25	-
	1986-87		28	14
Tr	1987-88	Notts Co	43	7
	1988-89		20	2
Tr	1989-90	Grimsby T	38	8
	1990-91		23	1
	1991-92		8	-

BONNYMAN, Philip

Glasgow, 6th February 1954

Source	Season	Club	Apps.	Gls
	1973-76	Hamilton Acad	71	7
Tr	1975-76	Carlisle U	9	-
	1976-77		37	1
	1977-78		33	8
	1978-79		45	7
	1979-80		28	10
Tr	1979-80	Chesterfield	11	3
	1980-81		42	8
	1981-82		46	14
Tr	1982-83	Grimsby T	40	1
	1983-84		29	3
	1984-85		37	8
	1985-86		29	3
L	1985-86	Stoke C	7	-
	1986-87	Grimsby T	16	-
Tr	1987-88	Darlington	38	3
	1988-89		12	2
Tr	1989-90	Dunfermline A	1	-

BURGESS, David J.

Liverpool, 20th January 1960

Source	Season	Club	Apps.	Gls
Local	1981-82	Tranmere R	46	1
	1982-83		46	-
	1983-84		44	-
	1984-85		41	-
	1985-86		41	-
Tr	1986-87	Grimsby T	31	-
	1987-88		38	-
Tr	1988-89	Blackpool	46	-
	1989-90		19	1
	1991-92		16	-
	1992-93		20	-

CALDWELL, Anthony

Salford, 21st March 1958

From Horwich RMI

Source	Season	Club	Apps.	Gls
	1983-84	Bolton W	33	19
	1984-85		31	18
	1985-86		40	10
	1986-87		35	11
Tr	1987-88	Bristol C	16	3
L	1987-88	Chester C	4	-
	1988-89	Bristol C	1	-
Tr	1988-89	Grimsby T	3	-
Tr	1988-89	Stockport Co	24	5
	1989-90		2	-

CHILDS, Gary P. C.

Birmingham, 19th April 1964

Source	Season	Club	Apps.	Gls
App	1981-82	West Brom A	2	-
	1982-83		-	-
	1983-84		1	-
Tr	1983-84	Walsall	30	2
	1984-85		40	2
	1985-86		33	5
	1986-87		28	8
Tr	1987-88	Birmingham C	32	1
	1988-89		23	1
Tr	1989-90	Grimsby T	44	5
	1990-91		25	4
	1991-92		29	3
	1992-93		16	-

COCKERILL, John

Cleethorpes, 12th July 1961

From Stafford Rangers

Source	Season	Club	Apps.	Gls
	1988-89	Grimsby T	29	6
	1989-90		33	5
	1990-91		35	7
	1991-92		10	1

COOPER, Neil

Aberdeen, 12th August 1959

From School

Source	Season	Club	Apps.	Gls
	1974-80	Aberdeen	12	1
Tr	1979-80	Barnsley	20	3
	1980-81		30	2
	1981-82		10	1
Tr	1981-82	Grimsby T	16	1
	1982-83		24	1
	1983-84		7	-
Tr	1983-89	St. Mirren	161	2
Tr	1989-90	Hibernian	27	-
	1990-91		11	-

CROFT, Gary

Burton, 17th February 1974

Source	Season	Club	Apps.	Gls
YT	1990-91	Grimsby T	1	-
	1991-92		-	-
	1992-93		32	-

CROMBIE, Dean M.

Lincoln, 9th August 1957

From Ruston Sports

Source	Season	Club	Apps.	Gls
	1976-77	Lincoln C	13	-
	1977-78		20	-
Tr	1978-79	Grimsby T	46	1
	1979-80		39	-
	1980-81		33	-
	1981-82		38	-
	1982-83		32	1
	1983-84		40	-
	1984-85		39	-

Source	Season	Club	Apps.	Gls
	1985-86	Grimsby T	34	1
	1986-87		19	-
L	1986-87	Reading	4	-
Tr	1987-88	Bolton W	24	-
	1988-89		31	-
	1989-90		38	1
	1990-91		2	-
Tr	1990-91	Lincoln C	1	-

CUMMING, Robert

Airdrie, 7th November 1955

From Baillieston Juniors

Source	Season	Club	Apps.	Gls
	1974-75	Grimsby T	5	-
	1975-76		32	2
	1976-77		41	-
	1977-78		27	3
	1978-79		34	9
	1979-80		40	14
	1980-81		32	11
	1981-82		24	2
	1982-83		33	7
	1983-84		30	1
	1984-85		20	5
	1985-86		24	2
	1986-87		23	1
Tr	1987-88	Lincoln C	33	7
	1988-89		29	5
	1989-90		12	-

CUNNINGTON, Shaun G.

Bourne, 4th January 1966

Source	Season	Club	Apps.	Gls
Jnrs	1982-83	Wrexham	4	-
	1983-84		42	-
	1984-85		41	6
	1985-86		42	2
	1986-87		46	1
	1987-88		24	3
Tr	1987-88	Grimsby T	15	2
	1988-89		44	1
	1989-90		44	3
	1990-91		46	2
	1991-92		33	5
Tr	1992-93	Sunderland	39	7

CURRAN, Edward (Terry)

Kinsley, 20th March 1955

Source	Season	Club	Apps.	Gls
Jnrs	1973-74	Doncaster R	22	2
	1974-75		44	7
	1975-76		2	2
Tr	1975-76	Nottingham F	33	6
	1976-77		15	6
L	1977-78	Bury	2	-
Tr	1977-78	Derby Co	26	2
Tr	1978-79	Southampton	26	-
Tr	1978-79	Sheffield W	12	1
	1979-80		41	22
	1981-82		36	9
Tr	1982-83	Sheffield U	33	3
L	1982-83	Everton	7	1

Source	Season	Club	Apps.	Gls
Tr	1983-84	Everton	8	-
	1984-85		9	-
Tr	1985-86	Huddersfield	34	7
Tr (PANIONIS) Greece				
	1986-87	Hull C	4	-
Tr	1986-87	Sunderland	9	1
From Grantham				
L	1987-88	Grimsby T	12	-
N/C	1987-88	Chesterfield	1	-

DAWS, Anthony

Sheffield, 10th September 1966

Source	Season	Club	Apps.	Gls
App	1984-85	Notts Co	7	1
	1985-86		1	-
Tr	1986-87	Sheffield U	11	3
Tr	1987-88	Scunthorpe U	10	3
	1988-89		46	24
	1989-90		33	11
	1990-91		34	14
	1991-92		36	7
	1992-93		24	4
Tr	1992-93	Grimsby T	6	1

DAWSON, Richard

Sheffield, 12th April 1967

Source	Season	Club	Apps.	Gls
Stoke C	1984-85	Grimsby T	1	-

DIXON, Andrew

Louth, 19th April 1968

Source	Season	Club	Apps.	Gls
App	1986-87	Grimsby T	1	-
	1987-88		32	-
	1988-89		5	-
Tr	1989-90	Southend U	24	-

DOBBIN, James

Dunfermline, 17th September 1963

Source	Season	Club	Apps.	Gls
Celtic	1983-84	Doncaster R	11	2
	1984-85		17	1
	1985-86		31	6
	1986-87		5	4
Tr	1986-87	Barnsley	30	4
	1987-88		16	2
	1988-89		41	5
	1989-90		28	1
	1990-91		14	-
Tr	1991-92	Grimsby T	32	6
	1992-93		39	5

DRINKELL, Kevin S.

Grimsby, 18th June 1960

Source	Season	Club	Apps.	Gls
App	1976-77	Grimsby T	4	2
	1977-78		26	5
	1978-79		28	7
	1979-80		33	16
	1980-81		41	7

Source	Season	Club	Apps.	Gls
	1981-82	Grimsby T	28	6
	1982-83		39	17
	1983-84		36	15
	1984-85		35	14
Tr	1985-86	Nowich C	41	22
	1986-87		42	16
	1987-88		38	12
Tr	1988-89	Glasgow Rangers	32	12
	1989-90		4	-
Tr	1989-90	Coventry C	22	5
	1990-91		15	-
	1991-92		4	-
L	1991-92	Birmingham C	5	2
Tr	1992-93	Falkirk (Player/Coach)		

EMSON, Paul D.

Lincoln, 22nd October 1958

Source	Season	Club	Apps.	Gls
Brigg T	1978-79	Derby Co	6	-
	1979-80		26	4
	1980-81		38	4
	1981-82		41	5
	1982-83		16	-
Tr	1983-84	Grimsby T	39	6
	1984-85		35	4
	1985-86		23	5
Tr	1986-87	Wrexham	35	3
	1987-88		14	2
Tr	1988-89	Darlington	34	5
	1989-90		34	7

FELGATE, David W.

Blaenau Ffestiniog, 4th March 1960

From Bolton Wanderers

Source	Season	Club	Apps.	Gls
L	1978-79	Rochdale	35	-
L	1979-80	Crewe A	14	-
L	1979-80	Rochdale	12	-
Tr	1980-81	Lincoln C	42	-
	1981-82		43	-
	1982-83		46	-
	1983-84		46	-
	1984-85		21	-
L	1984-85	Cardiff C	4	-
L	1984-85	Grimsby T	12	-
Tr	1985-86	Grimsby T	12	-
Tr	1985-86	Bolton W	15	-
	1986-87		20	-
	1987-88		46	-
	1988-89		46	-
	1989-90		40	-
	1990-91		46	-
	1991-92		25	-
	1992-93		-	-

FOLEY, Steven

Liverpool, 4th October 1962

From Apprentice, Liverpool

Source	Season	Club	Apps.	Gls
L	1983-84	Fulham	3	-
Tr	1984-85	Grimsby T	31	2
Tr	1985-86	Sheffield U	28	5

Source	Season	Club	Apps.	Gls
	1986-87		38	9
Tr	1987-88	Swindon T	35	4
	1988-89		40	8
	1989-90		23	4
	1990-91		44	7
	1991-92		9	-
Tr	1991-92	Stoke C	20	1
	1992-93		44	7

FORD, Tony

Grimsby, 14th May 1959

Source	Season	Club	Apps.	Gls
App	1975-76	Grimsby T	14	-
	1976-77		6	-
	1977-78		34	2
	1978-79		45	15
	1979-80		37	5
	1980-81		28	4
	1981-82		35	7
	1982-83		37	4
	1983-84		42	8
	1984-85		42	6
	1985-86		34	3
L	1985-86	Sunderland	9	1
Tr	1986-87	Stoke C	41	6
	1987-88		44	7
	1988-89		27	-
Tr	1988-89	West Brom A	11	1
	1989-90		42	8
	1990-91		46	5
	1991-92		15	-
Tr	1991-92	Grimsby T	22	1
	1992-93		17	2

FUTCHER, Paul

Chester, 25th September 1956

Source	Season	Club	Apps.	Gls
App	1972-73	Chester	2	-
	1973-74		18	-
Tr	1974-75	Luton T	19	-
	1975-76		41	-
	1976-77		40	1
	1977-78		31	-
Tr	1978-79	Manchester C	24	-
	1979-80		13	-
Tr	1980-81	Oldham A	36	1
	1981-82		37	-
	1982-83		25	-
Tr	1982-83	Derby Co	17	-
	1983-84		18	-
Tr	1983-84	Barnsley	10	-
	1984-85		36	-
	1985-86		37	-
	1986-87		36	-
	1987-88		41	-
	1988-89		41	-
	1989-90		29	-
Tr	1990-91	Halifax T	15	-
Tr	1990-91	Grimsby T	22	-
	1991-92		29	-
	1992-93		35	-

GABBIADINI, Riccardo

Newport, 11th March 1970

Source	Season	Club	Apps.	Gls
YT	1987-88	York C	1	-
Tr	1988-89	Sunderland	-	-
	1989-90		1	-
L	1989-90	Blackpool	5	3
L	1989-90	Brighton & HA	1	-
L	1989-90	Grimsby T	3	1
L	1990-91	Crewe Alex	2	-
Tr	1990-91	Hartlepool U	5	-
	1991-92		9	2
Tr	1991-92	Scarborough	7	1
Tr	1992-93	Carlisle U	24	3

GILBERT, David J.

Lincoln, 22nd June 1963

Source	Season	Club	Apps.	Gls
App	1980-81	Lincoln C	1	-
	1981-82		29	1
Tr	1982-83	Scunthorpe U	1	-
From Boston U				
Tr	1986-87	Northampton T	45	8
	1987-88		41	6
	1988-89		34	7
Tr	1988-89	Grimsby T	11	3
	1989-90		45	10
	1990-91		44	12
	1991-92		41	2
	1992-93		41	4

GILLIGAN, James M.

Hammersmith, 24th January 1964

Source	Season	Club	Apps.	Gls
App	1981-82	Watford	1	-
	1982-83		4	2
L	1982-83	Lincoln C	3	-
	1983-84	Watford	12	4
	1984-85		10	-
Tr	1985-86	Grimsby T	25	4
Tr	1986-87	Swindon T	17	5
L	1986-87	Newport Co	5	1
Tr	1986-87	Lincoln C	11	1
Tr	1987-88	Cardiff C	46	19
	1988-89		46	15
	1989-90		7	1
Tr	1989-90	Portsmouth	32	15
Tr	1990-91	Swansea C	37	16
	1991-92		25	7

GROCOCK, Christopher R.

Grimsby, 30th October 1968

Source	Season	Club	Apps.	Gls
Jnrs	1985-86	Grimsby T	1	-
	1986-87		6	-

GROTIER, Peter D.

Stratford, 18th October 1950

Source	Season	Club	Apps.	Gls
App	1968-69	West Ham U	2	-
	1969-70		12	-

Source	Season	Club	Apps.	Gls
	1970-71		19	-
	1971-72		6	-
	1972-73		11	-
L	1973-74	Cardiff C	2	-
Tr	1974-75	Lincoln C	46	-
	1975-76		46	-
	1976-77		44	-
	1977-78		44	-
	1978-79		32	-
	1979-80		21	-
Tr	1979-80	Cardiff C	7	-
	1980-81		22	-
	1981-82		9	-
Tr	1982-83	Grimsby T	4	-
	1983-84		6	-

GROVES, Paul

Derby, 28th February 1966

From Burton Albion

Source	Season	Club	Apps.	Gls
	1987-88	Leicester C	1	1
	1988-89		15	-
L	1989-90	Lincoln C	8	1
Tr	1989-90	Blackpool	19	1
	1990-91		46	11
	1991-92		42	9
Tr	1992-93	Grimsby T	46	12

HALSALL, Michael

Bootle, 21st July 1961

From Apprentice, Liverpool

Source	Season	Club	Apps.	Gls
Tr	1982-83	Birmingham C	12	1
	1983-84		21	2
	1984-85		3	-
Tr	1984-85	Carlisle U	26	5
	1985-86		41	4
	1986-87		25	2
Tr	1986-87	Grimsby T	12	-
Tr	1987-88	Peterborough U	45	4
	1988-89		42	1
	1989-90		46	10
	1990-91		45	6
	1991-92		45	5
	1992-93		25	-

HANDYSIDE, Peter

Dumfries, 31st July 1974

Source	Season	Club	Apps.	Gls
YT	1992-93	Grimsby T	11	-

HARGREAVES, Christian

Cleethorpes, 12th May 1972

Source	Season	Club	Apps.	Gls
YT	1989-90	Grimsby T	19	2
	1990-91		18	3
	1991-92		10	-
	1992-93		4	-
L	1992-93	Scarborough	3	-

Source	Season	Club	Apps.	Gls

HAZEL, Desmond L.

Bradford, 15th July 1967

From Apprentice, Sheffield Wednesday

Source	Season	Club	Apps.	Gls
L	1986-87	Grimsby T	9	2
	1987-88	Sheffield W	6	-
Tr	1988-89	Rotherham U	42	6
	1989-90		33	2
	1990-91		39	3
	1991-92		38	8
	1992-93		36	6

HENSHAW, Gary

Leeds, 18th February 1965

Source	Season	Club	Apps.	Gls
App	1983-84	Grimsby T	4	-
	1984-85		7	1
	1985-86		10	4
	1986-87		29	4
Tr	1987-88	Bolton W	31	2
	1988-89		21	2
	1989-90		14	-
L	1989-90	Rochdale	9	1
	1990-91	Bolton W	4	-

HINE, Mark

Middlesbrough, 18th May 1964

From Whitby Town

Source	Season	Club	Apps.	Gls
	1984-85	Grimsby T	9	-
	1985-86		13	1
Tr	1986-87	Darlington	43	2
	1987-88		45	4
	1988-89		40	2
Tr	1989-90	Peterborough U	22	4
	1990-91		33	4
Tr	1990-91	Scunthorpe U	12	2
	1991-92		10	-
Tr	1992-93	Doncaster R	25	1

HOBSON, Gordon

Sheffield, 27th November 1957

From Sheffield R.

Source	Season	Club	Apps.	Gls
	1977-78	Lincoln C	5	2
	1978-79		33	6
	1979-80		43	10
	1980-81		44	21
	1981-82		32	7
	1982-83		41	14
	1983-84		36	6
	1984-85		38	7
Tr	1985-86	Grimsby T	41	15
	1986-87		11	3
Tr	1986-87	Southampton	20	7
	1987-88		13	1
Tr	1988-89	Lincoln C	32	14
	1989-90		29	8
Tr	1990-91	Exeter C	37	7
	1991-92		1	-
Tr	1991-92	Walsall	3	-

HORWOOD, Neil K.

Peterhead, 4th August 1964

From Kings Lynn

Source	Season	Club	Apps.	Gls
	1986-87	Grimsby T	1	-
L	1986-87	Halifax T	3	-
L	1986-87	Tranmere R	4	1
Tr	1987-88	Cambridge U (N/C)	14	2

JOBLING, Kevin A.

Sunderland, 1st January 1968

Source	Season	Club	Apps.	Gls
App	1986-87	Leicester C	3	-
	1987-88		6	-
Tr	1987-88	Grimsby T	15	1
	1988-89		32	4
	1989-90		33	1
	1990-91		45	-
	1991-92		36	2
	1992-93		14	-

JONES, Murray L.

Bexley, 7th October 1964

From Apprentice, Southend. Then Carshalton Athletic

Source	Season	Club	Apps.	Gls
	1989-90	Crystal Palace	-	-
Tr	1990-91	Bristol C	-	-
L	1990-91	Doncaster R	-	-
Tr	1990-91	Exeter C	20	3
Tr	1991-92	Grimsby T	28	3
Tr	1992-93	Brentford	16	-

KNIGHT, Ian J.

Hartlepool, 26th October 1966

From Apprentice, Barnsley

Source	Season	Club	Apps.	Gls
Tr	1985-86	Sheffield W	4	-
	1986-87		15	-
	1988-89		2	-
L	1989-90	Scunthorpe U	2	-
Tr	1989-90	Grimsby T	9	1
	1990-91		8	1
	1991-92		4	-

LEVER, Mark

Beverley, 29th March 1970

Source	Season	Club	Apps.	Gls
YT	1987-88	Grimsby T	1	-
	1988-89		37	2
	1989-90		38	2
	1990-91		40	2
	1991-92		36	-
	1992-93		14	1

LUND, Gary J.

Grimsby, 13th September 1964

Source	Season	Club	Apps.	Gls
YT	1983-84	Grimsby T	7	4
	1984-85		24	12
	1985-86		29	8

Source	Season	Club	Apps.	Gls
Tr	1986-87	Lincoln C	44	13
Tr	1987-88	Notts Co	40	20
	1988-89		42	8
	1989-90		40	9
	1990-91		16	3
	1991-92		13	2
	1992-93		28	4

LYONS, Michael
Liverpool, 8th December 1951

Source	Season	Club	Apps.	Gls
App	1970-71	Everton	2	1
	1971-72		24	3
	1972-73		25	2
	1973-74		41	9
	1974-75		38	8
	1975-76		42	5
	1976-77		40	4
	1977-78		42	5
	1978-79		37	6
	1979-80		39	-
	1980-81		33	2
	1981-82		27	3
Tr	1982-83	Sheffield W	39	3
	1983-84		42	5
	1984-85		37	3
	1985-86		11	1
Tr	1986-87	Grimsby T	24	4

MATTHEWS, Neil
Grimsby, 19th September 1966

Source	Season	Club	Apps.	Gls
App	1984-85	Grimsby T	4	1
	1985-86		4	-
L	1985-86	Scunthorpe U	1	-
	1986-87	Grimsby T	3	-
L	1986-87	Halifax T	9	2
L	1986-87	Bolton W	1	-
Tr	1987-88	Halifax T	32	10
	1988-89		34	7
	1989-90		39	12
Tr	1990-91	Stockport Co	29	14
	1991-92		9	1
L	1991-92	Halifax T	3	-
	1992-93	Stockport Co	5	-
Tr	1992-93	Lincoln C	24	12

MENDONCA, Clive P
Islington, 9th September 1968

Source	Season	Club	Apps.	Gls
App	1986-87	Sheffield U	2	-
	1987-88		11	4
L	1987-88	Doncaster R	2	-
Tr	1987-88	Rotherham U	8	2
	1988-89		10	1
	1989-90		32	14
	1990-91		34	10
Tr	1991-92	Sheffield U	10	1
L	1991-92	Grimsby T	10	3
Tr	1992-93		42	10

MOORE, Andrew R.
Cleethorpes, 14th November 1965

Source	Season	Club	Apps.	Gls
App	1983-84	Grimsby T	9	-
	1984-85		13	-
	1985-86		33	1

MOORE, David
Grimsby, 17th December 1959

Source	Season	Club	Apps.	Gls
App	1978-79	Grimsby T	30	-
	1979-80		29	-
	1980-81		5	-
	1981-82		34	2
	1982-83		38	-
Tr	1983-84	Carlisle U	13	1
Tr	1983-84	Blackpool	28	1
	1984-85		44	-
	1985-86		41	-
	1986-87		2	-
Tr	1986-87	Grimsby T	3	-
	1987-88		1	-
Tr	1988-89	Darlington	30	1

MOORE, Kevin T.
Grimsby, 29th April 1958

Source	Season	Club	Apps.	Gls
Jnrs	1976-77	Grimsby T	28	-
	1977-78		42	-
	1978-79		46	6
	1979-80		41	4
	1980-81		41	1
	1981-82		36	4
	1982-83		38	-
	1983-84		41	1
	1984-85		31	4
	1985-86		31	2
	1986-87		25	5
Tr	1986-87	Oldham A	13	1
Tr	1987-88	Southampton	35	3
	1988-89		25	3
	1989-90		21	1
	1990-91		19	1
	1991-92		16	-
L	1991-92	Bristol R	7	-
	1992-93	Southampton	13	2
L	1992-93	Bristol R	4	-

McDERMOTT, John
Middlesbrough, 3rd February 1969

Source	Season	Club	Apps.	Gls
YT	1986-87	Grimsby T	13	-
	1987-88		28	-
	1988-89		38	1
	1989-90		39	-
	1990-91		43	-
	1991-92		39	1
	1992-93		38	2

45

Source	Season	Club	Apps.	Gls
	1980-81	Walsall	38	7
	1981-82		29	6
	1982-83		35	7
	1983-84		40	12
	1984-85		34	16
	1985-86		28	8
Tr	1986-87	Port Vale	12	3
	1987-88		16	1
Tr	1987-88	Walsall	12	1
Tr	1988-89	Grimsby T	39	10

McGARVEY, Scott T.

Glasgow, 22nd April 1963

Source	Season	Club	Apps.	Gls
App	1980-81	Manchester U	2	-
	1981-82		16	2
	1982-83		7	1
L	1983-84	Wolverhampton W	13	2
Tr	1984-85	Portsmouth	18	5
	1985-86		5	1
L	1985-86	Carlisle U	10	3
Tr	1986-87	Carlisle U	25	8
Tr	1986-87	Grimsby T	11	1
	1987-88		39	6
Tr	1988-89	Bristol C	26	9
Tr	1989-90	Oldham A	4	1
L	1989-90	Wigan A	3	-

To Mazda, Japan

NICHOLL, Christopher J.

Wilmslow, 12th October 1946

From Witton Albion

Source	Season	Club	Apps.	Gls
	1968-69	Halifax T	42	3
	1969-70	Luton T	27	2
	1970-71		39	1
	1971-72		32	3
Tr	1971-72	Aston Villa	13	1
	1972-73		41	-
	1973-74		40	-
	1974-75		41	4
	1975-76		40	4
	1976-77		35	2
Tr	1977-78	Southampton	39	1
	1978-79		38	3
	1979-80		33	1
	1980-81		42	3
	1981-82		34	-
	1982-83		42	-
Tr	1983-84	Grimsby T	39	-

NORTH, Marcus V.

Ware, 29th May 1966

From Apprentice. Luton Town

Source	Season	Club	Apps.	Gls
L	1984-85	Lincoln C	4	-
	1985-86	Luton T	13	3
	1986-87		5	-
L	1986-87	Scunthorpe U	5	2
L	1986-87	Birmingham C	5	1
Tr	1987-88	Grimsby T	38	11
	1988-89		29	6
Tr	1988-89	Leicester C	8	1
	1989-90		24	6
	1990-91		39	2

From Luton Town (N/C)

Source	Season	Club	Apps.	Gls
L	1991-92	Grimsby T	1	-

O'KELLY, Richard F.

West Bromwich, 8th January 1957

From Alvechurch

O'RIORDAN, Donal J.

Dublin, 14th May 1957

Source	Season	Club	Apps.	Gls
App	1976-77	Derby Co	1	-
	1977-78		5	1
L	1977-78	Doncaster R	2	-
Tulsa H	1978-79	Preston NE	32	-
	1979-80		18	-
	1980-81		21	-
	1981-82		46	4
	1982-83		41	4
Tr	1983-84	Carlisle U	42	8
	1984-85		42	10
Tr	1985-86	Middlesbrough	41	2
Tr	1986-87	Grimsby T	40	6
	1987-88		46	8
Tr	1988-89	Notts Co	43	3
L	1989-90	Mansfield T	6	-
	1990-91	Notts Co	31	1
	1991-92		1	-
	1992-93		17	1
Tr	1992-93	Torquay U	16	-

PEAKE, Andrew M.

Market Harborough, 1st November 1961

Source	Season	Club	Apps.	Gls
App	1978-79	Leicester C	18	2
	1979-80		25	3
	1980-81		24	1
	1981-82		31	2
	1982-83		4	-
	1983-84		24	4
	1984-85		21	1
Tr	1985-86	Grimsby T	36	4
	1986-87		3	-
Tr	1986-87	Charlton A	29	-
	1987-88		16	-
	1988-89		31	1
	1989-90		36	-
	1990-91		45	4
	1991-92		20	-
Tr	1991-92	Middlesbrough	23	-
	1992-93		26	-

PRATT, Lee S.

Cleethorpes, 31st March 1970

Source	Season	Club	Apps.	Gls
YT	1986-87	Grimsby T	1	-

PRUDHOE, Mark

Washington, 11th November 1963

Source	Season	Club	Apps.	Gls
App	1982-83	Sunderland	7	-
L	1983-84	Hartlepool U	3	-
Tr	1984-85	Birmingham C	1	-
Tr	1985-86	Walsall	16	-
	1986-87		10	-
L	1986-87	Doncaster R	5	-
L	1986-87	Grimsby T	8	-
L	1987-88	Hartlepool U	13	-
L	1987-88	Bristol C	3	-
Tr	1987-88	Carlisle U	22	-
Tr	1988-89	Darlington	12	-
	1989-90		34	-
	1990-91		46	-
	1991-92		46	-
	1992-93		42	-

RAWCLIFFE, Peter

Cleethorpes, 6th December 1963

Source	Season	Club	Apps.	Gls
Louth U	1986-87	Grimsby T	20	2
	1987-88		2	-
From King's Lynn				
	1990-91	Lincoln C	1	-

REECE, Paul J.

Nottingham, 16th August 1968

From Apprentice, Stoke City then Kettering Town

Source	Season	Club	Apps.	Gls
	1988-89	Grimsby T	14	-
	1989-90		15	-
	1991-92		25	-
L	1992-93	Doncaster R	1	-
Tr	1992-93	Oxford U	35	-

REES, Anthony A.

Merthyr Tydfil, 1st August 1964

From Apprentice, Aston Villa

Source	Season	Club	Apps.	Gls
Tr	1983-84	Birmingham C	25	2
	1984-85		9	2
	1985-86		8	-
L	1985-86	Peterborough U	5	2
L	1985-86	Shrewsbury T	2	-
	1986-87	Birmingham C	30	4
	1987-88		23	4
Tr	1987-88	Barnsley	14	2
	1988-89		17	1
Tr	1989-90	Grimsby T	35	13
	1990-91		36	10
	1991-92		23	5
	1992-93		31	5

RICE, Brian

Bellshill, 11th October 1963

From Hibernian

Source	Season	Club	Apps.	Gls
	1985-86	Nottingham F	19	3
	1986-87		3	1

Source	Season	Club	Apps.	Gls
L	1986-87	Grimsby T	4	-
	1987-88	Nottingham F	30	2
	1988-89		20	1
L	1988-89	West Brom A	3	-
	1989-90	Nottingham F	18	2
	1990-91		1	-
L	1990-91	Stoke C	18	-
Tr	1991-92	Falkirk	16	1

ROBINSON, Neil

Liverpool, 20th April 1957

Source	Season	Club	Apps.	Gls
App	1975-76	Everton	1	-
	1976-77		4	-
	1977-78		4	1
	1978-79		7	-
Tr	1979-80	Swansea C	16	-
	1980-81		36	6
	1981-82		29	1
	1982-83		18	-
	1983-84		19	-
	1984-85		5	-
Tr	1984-85	Grimsby T	17	-
	1985-86		22	-
	1986-87		30	3
	1987-88		40	3
Tr	1988-89	Darlington	38	1

RODGER, Graham

Glasgow, 1st April 1967

Source	Season	Club	Apps.	Gls
App	1983-84	Wolverhampton W	1	-
Tr (84/5)	1985-86	Coventry C	10	-
	1986-87		6	-
	1987-88		12	1
	1988-89		8	1
Tr	1989-90	Luton T	2	-
	1990-91		14	2
	1991-92		12	-
Tr	1991-92	Grimsby T	12	-
	1992-93		30	7

ROWBOTHAM, Michael G.

Sheffield, 2nd September 1965

Source	Season	Club	Apps.	Gls
App	1983-84	Manchester U	-	-
Tr	1984-85	Grimsby T	4	-

SAUNDERS, Steven J. P.

Warrington, 21st September 1964

Source	Season	Club	Apps.	Gls
App	1983-84	Bolton W	3	-
Tr	1985-86	Crewe Alex	22	1
Tr	1986-87	Preston NE	-	-
Tr	1987-88	Grimsby T	35	3
	1988-89	Grimsby T	41	10
Tr	1989-90	Scarborough	32	1

Source	Season	Club	Apps.	Gls

SEAGRAVES, Christopher A.

Liverpool, 7th October 1964

Source	Season	Club	Apps.	Gls
App	1983-84	Liverpool	-	-
Tr	1984-85	Grimsby	23	-

SHEARER, David J.

Inverness, 16th October 1958

From Inverness Clachnacuddin

Source	Season	Club	Apps.	Gls
	1977-78	Middlesbrough	4	2
	1978-79		5	1
	1979-80		5	1
L	1979-80	Wigan A	11	9
	1980-81	Middlesbrough	30	7
	1981-82		24	3
	1982-83		29	9
Tr	1983-84	Grimsby T	4	-
Tr	1984-85	Gillingham	23	12
	1985-86		23	9
	1986-87		36	16
	1987-88		11	5
Tr	1987-88	Bournemouth	11	3
Tr	1987-88	Scunthorpe U	15	7
	1988-89		1	-
Tr	1988-89	Darlington	7	-

SHERWOOD, Stephen

Selby, 10th December 1953

Source	Season	Club	Apps.	Gls
App	1971-72	Chelsea	1	-
	1972-73		3	-
L	1973-74	Millwall	1	-
L	1973-74	Brentford	16	-
L	1974-75		46	-
	1975-76	Chelsea	12	-
Tr	1976-77	Watford	8	-
	1977-78		16	-
	1978-79		16	-
	1979-80		4	-
	1980-81		22	-
	1981-82		41	-
	1982-83		42	-
	1983-84		40	1
	1984-85		9	-
	1985-86		2	-
	1986-87		11	-
Tr	1987-88	Grimsby T	46	-
	1988-89		32	-
	1989-90		31	-
	1990-91		46	-
	1991-92		21	-
	1992-93		7	-

SLACK, Trevor C.

Peterborough, 26th September 1962

Source	Season	Club	Apps.	Gls
App	1980-81	Peterborough U	35	4
	1981-82		7	2
	1982-83		40	1
	1983-84		39	3

Source	Season	Club	Apps.	Gls
	1984-85		41	3
	1985-86		40	5
Tr	1986-87	Rotherham U	15	1
Tr	1987-88	Grimsby T	21	-
Tr	1987-88	Northampton T	13	1
Tr	1988-89	Chesterfield	21	-
	1989-90		2	-

SMALLER, Paul A.

Scunthorpe, 18th September 1970

Source	Season	Club	Apps.	Gls
YT	1988-89	Grimsby T	1	-

SMITH, Mark C.

Sheffield, 19th December 1961

From Gainsborough Trinity

Source	Season	Club	Apps.	Gls
	1985-86	Scunthorpe U	1	-

From Kettering

Source	Season	Club	Apps.	Gls
	1988-89	Rochdale	27	7
Tr	1988-89	Huddersfield T	20	2
	1989-90		44	7
	1990-91		32	2
Tr	1990-91	Grimsby T	11	-
	1991-92		40	4
	1992-93		26	-

SPEIGHT, Michael

Upton, 1st November 1951

Source	Season	Club	Apps.	Gls
App	1971-72	Sheffield U	4	-
	1972-73		9	-
	1973-74		24	1
	1974-75		33	2
	1975-76		19	-
	1976-77		3	-
	1977-78		33	3
	1978-79		39	2
	1979-80		35	6
Tr	1980-81	Blackburn R	38	4
	1981-82		13	-
Tr	1982-83	Grimsby T	13	-
L	1982-83	Bury	-	-
	1983-84	Grimsby T	25	2
Tr	1984-85	Chester C	30	1
	1985-86		10	-

STEPHENSON, Geoffrey

Tynemouth, 28th April 1970

Source	Season	Club	Apps.	Gls
YT	1988-89	Grimsby T	14	-

STOUTT, Stephen P.

Halifax, 5th April 1964

From Bradley R.

Source	Season	Club	Apps.	Gls
	1983-84	Huddersfield T	3	-
	1984-85		3	-
Tr (84/5)	1985-86	Wolverhampton W	28	-
	1986-87		44	4
	1987-88		22	1

Source	Season	Club	Apps.	Gls
Tr	1988-89	Grimsby T	2	1
	1989-90		1	-
Tr	1989-90	Lincoln C	21	-

STRAW, Ian E.

Sheffield, 27th May 1967

From Apprentice, Southampton

Source	Season	Club	Apps.	Gls
L	1986-87	Grimsby T	10	-

STUBBS, William (Billy)

Hartlepool, 1st August 1966

From Seaham Red Star

Source	Season	Club	Apps.	Gls
	1986-87	Nottingham F	-	-
L	1987-88	Doncaster R	9	1
L	1987-88	Grimsby T	7	2

TILLSON, Andrew

Huntingdon, 30th July 1966

From Kettering

Source	Season	Club	Apps.	Gls
	1988-89	Grimsby T	45	2
	1989-90		42	3
	1990-91		18	-
Tr	1990-91	QPR	19	2
	1991-92		10	-
	1992-93		-	-
L	1992-93	Grimsby T	4	-
Tr	1992-93	Bristol R	29	-

TOALE, Ian

Liverpool, 28th August 1967

Source	Season	Club	Apps.	Gls
App	1986-87	Liverpool	-	-
Tr	1987-88	Grimsby T	20	-

TURNER, Philip

Sheffield, 12th February 1962

Source	Season	Club	Apps.	Gls
App	1979-80	Lincoln C	14	1
	1980-81		38	4
	1981-82		28	1
	1982-83		40	3
	1983-84		42	3
	1984-85		36	3
	1985-86		43	4
Tr	1986-87	Grimsby T	34	3
	1987-88		28	5
Tr	1987-88	Leicester C	8	-
	1988-89		16	2
Tr	1988-89	Notts Co	16	2
	1989-90		44	6
	1990-91		38	1
	1991-92		29	1
	1992-93		20	-

WALSH, Ian P.

St. Davids, 4th September 1958

Source	Season	Club	Apps.	Gls
App	1976-77	Crystal Palace	1	-
	1977-78		16	2
	1978-79		33	8
	1979-80		29	6
	1980-81		25	5
	1981-82		13	2
Tr	1981-82	Swansea C	5	2
	1982-83		8	3
	1983-84		24	6
Tr	1984-85	Barnsley	16	-
	1985-86		33	15
Tr	1986-87	Grimsby T	30	9
	1987-88		11	5
Tr	1987-88	Cardiff C	6	-
	1988-89		11	4

WATERS, Joseph W.

Limerick, 20th September 1953

Source	Season	Club	Apps.	Gls
App	1973-74	Leicester C	8	1
	1974-75		5	-
Tr	1975-76	Grimsby T	19	2
	1976-77		45	6
	1977-78		46	8
	1978-79		46	10
	1979-80		46	7
	1980-81		42	10
	1981-82		36	7
	1982-83		40	8
	1983-84		37	7

WATSON, Thomas R.

Liverpool, 29th September 1969

Source	Season	Club	Apps.	Gls
YT	1987-88	Grimsby T	19	-
	1988-89		21	4
	1989-90		16	1
	1990-91		41	9
	1991-92		17	2
	1992-93		24	4

WHYMARK, Trevor J.

Burston, 4th May 1950

Source	Season	Club	Apps.	Gls
Diss T.	1969-70	Ipswich T	8	1
	1970-71		10	1
	1971-72		13	3
	1972-73		41	11
	1973-74		39	11
	1974-75		40	10
	1975-76		40	13
	1976-77		36	14
	1977-78		20	9
	1978-79		13	1

From Sparta Rotterdam

Source	Season	Club	Apps.	Gls
	1979-80	Derby Co	2	-

From Vancouver

Source	Season	Club	Apps.	Gls
	1980-81	Grimsby T	21	3

Source	Season	Club	Apps.	Gls
	1981-82	Grimsby T	33	11
	1982-83		28	1
	1983-84		11	1
Tr	1983-84	Southend U	19	3
	1984-85		19	2
Tr	1985-86	Peterborough U	3	-
(N/C)	1985-86	Colchester U	2	-

WILKINSON, Paul

Louth, 30th October 1964

Source	Season	Club	Apps.	Gls
App	1982-83	Grimsby T	4	1
	1983-84		37	12
	1984-85		30	14
Tr	1984-85	Everton	5	2
	1985-86		4	1
	1986-87		22	4
Tr	1986-87	Nottingham F	8	-
	1987-88		26	5
Tr	1988-89	Watford	45	19
	1989-90		43	15
	1990-91		46	18
Tr	1991-92	Middlesbrough	46	15
	1992-93		41	14

WILLIAMS, Thomas E.

Winchburgh, 18th December 1957

Source	Season	Club	Apps.	Gls
App	1977-78	Leicester C	32	3
	1978-79		35	2
	1979-80		40	1
	1980-81		42	4
	1981-82		31	-
	1982-83		4	-
	1983-84		22	-
	1984-85		27	-
	1985-86		8	-
Tr	1986-87	Birmingham C	29	-
	1987-88		33	1
Tr	1988-89	Grimsby T	19	-

WILLIS, Roger C. (Harry)

Sheffield, 17th June 1967

Source	Season	Club	Apps.	Gls
Dunkirk	1989-90	Grimsby T	9	-
Tr	1991-92	Barnet	38	12
	1992-93		6	-
Tr	1992-93	Watford	32	2

WILMOT, Rhys

Newport, 21st February 1962

From Apprentice, Arsenal

Source	Season	Club	Apps.	Gls
L	1982-83	Hereford U	9	-
L	1984-85	Orient	46	-
	1985-86	Arsenal	2	-
	1986-87		6	-
L	1988-89	Swansea C	16	-
L	1988-89	Plymouth A	17	-
Tr	1989-90	Plymouth A	46	-
	1990-91		36	-

Source	Season	Club	Apps.	Gls
	1991-92		34	-
Tr	1992-93	Grimsby T	33	-

WOODS, Neil S.

York, 30th July 1966

Source	Season	Club	Apps.	Gls
App	1982-83	Doncaster R	4	-
	1983-84		7	1
	1984-85		6	2
	1985-86		30	7
	1986-87		18	6
Tr	1986-87	Glasgow Rangers	3	-
Tr	1987-88	Ipswich T	19	4
	1988-89		1	-
	1989-90		7	1
Tr	1989-90	Bradford C	14	2
Tr	1990-91	Grimsby T	44	12
	1991-92		37	8
	1992-93		30	3

Ian Walsh (played for town 1986-88). Signed on a free transfer from Barnsley in August 1986. Top Scorer in 1986-87 season (9 goals)

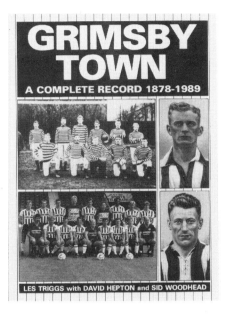
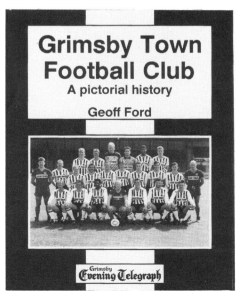

Supporters' Guides : -

THE SUPPORTERS' GUIDE TO PREMIER & FOOTBALL LEAGUE CLUBS 1994

Featuring :
- all Premier League Clubs
- all Football League clubs
+ 1992/93 season's Results & Tables
120 pages - price £4.99 - post free

THE SUPPORTERS' GUIDE TO NON-LEAGUE FOOTBALL 1994

Featuring :
- all GM/Vauxhall Conference clubs
- all HFS Loans - Premier clubs
- all Beazer Homes - Premier clubs
- all Diadora Premier clubs
+ 180 other major Non-League clubs
112 pages - price £4.99 - post free

THE SUPPORTERS' GUIDE TO SCOTTISH FOOTBALL 1994

Featuring :
- all Scottish League clubs
- all Highland League clubs
- all East of Scotland League clubs
+ Results, tables
96 pages - price £4.99 - post free

THE SUPPORTERS' GUIDE TO WELSH FOOTBALL 1994

Featuring :
- all Konica League of Wales clubs
- all Cymru Alliance & Abacus League clubs
+ 'The Exiles', Minor League clubs & 1992/93 season's results and tables
96 pages - price £4.99 - post free

order from : -

**SOCCER BOOK PUBLISHING LTD.
72 ST. PETERS AVENUE
CLEETHORPES
DN35 8HU
ENGLAND**